PENGUIN BOOKS

Cosmopolitan Guide to Working i

Robert Gray is a freelance journalist who contributes to consumer magazines, national newspapers and the business press. He is author of the *Cosmopolitan Guide to Working in Finance*, which is also available in Penguin.

Julia Hobsbawm is a member of the Institute of Public Relations. Her PR career began in 1984, working for various publishers, including Penguin Books. She has been described by *The Times* magazine as 'one of the most sensible and intelligent publicists around', and her agency, Hobsbawm Macaulay Communications Limited, has offices in Edinburgh and New York. This is her first book.

COSMOPOLITAN
Guide to Working in **PR** and **Advertising**

ROBERT GRAY AND JULIA HOBSBAWM

PENGUIN BOOKS

PENGUIN BOOKS

Published by the Penguin Group
Penguin Books Ltd, 27 Wrights Lane, London w8 5tz, England
Penguin Books USA Inc., 375 Hudson Street, New York, New York 10014, USA
Penguin Books Australia Ltd, Ringwood, Victoria, Australia
Penguin Books Canada Ltd, 10 Alcorn Avenue, Toronto, Ontario, Canada m4v 3b2
Penguin Books (NZ) Ltd, 182–190 Wairau Road, Auckland 10, New Zealand

Penguin Books Ltd, Registered Offices: Harmondsworth, Middlesex, England

First published 1996
10 9 8 7 6 5 4 3 2 1

Copyright © The National Magazine Company, 1996
All rights reserved

The moral right of the authors has been asserted

The expression *Cosmopolitan* is the trade mark of The National Magazine
Company Limited and The Hearst Corporation, registered in the UK and the
USA, and other principal countries of the world, and is the absolute property of
The National Magazine Company Limited and The Hearst Corporation. The use
of this trademark other than with the express permission of The National
Magazine Company or The Hearst Corporation is strictly prohibited

Set in 10.5/13 pt Monotype Baskerville
Typeset by Datix International Limited, Bungay, Suffolk
Printed in England by Clays Ltd, St Ives plc

Except in the United States of America, this book is sold subject
to the condition that it shall not, by way of trade or otherwise, be lent,
re-sold, hired out, or otherwise circulated without the publisher's
prior consent in any form of binding or cover other than that in
which it is published and without a similar condition including this
condition being imposed on the subsequent purchaser

Contents

Acknowledgements vii

Chapter 1 / **Introduction** 1

Chapter 2 / **What is PR?** 7

Chapter 3 / **Working in PR** 26

Chapter 4 / **Specialist PR** 52

Chapter 5 / **Advertising Agencies** 71

Chapter 6 / **Advertising from the Client's Side** 95

Chapter 7 / **Media** 113

Chapter 8 / **Personal Qualities** 133

Chapter 9 / **Qualifications and Courses** 134

Chapter 10 / **Guide to the Jargon** 144

Chapter 11 / **Getting a Job** 156

Chapter 12 / **Further Information** 178

Chapter 13 / **Further Reading** 184

Acknowledgements

The authors would like to thank the following people for their help and support with this book: Suzanne King, series editor; Emma Dally at National Magazine Company; our editor, Liz Halsall at Penguin; and all those who took part in interviews and responded to our research questions.

Julia Hobsbawm: I would like to thank the following people: Ruth Dunitz for originally setting the standard; Andrew Franklin for wanting to publish this book in the first place; Shanna Benjamin; Karen Brown, Ann Geneva and Hazel Petherick for research; Jeremy Weinberg at the Institute of Public Relations and Jessica Morris at Fishburn Hedges for reading the manuscript and providing comments; and, finally, many thanks to everyone at Hobsbawm Macaulay Communications Ltd, especially Sarah Macaulay.

Robert Gray: My thanks to Miranda Kennett at the IPA, and to the Advertising Association and *Financial Times* for putting their libraries at my disposal. Finally, special thanks to my wife Liz for her encouragement and support.

Chapter 1 / **Introduction**

The words public relations and advertising may conjure up a glamorous image in your mind: lavish parties, long lunches, glitzy launches and foreign 'shoots' at someone else's expense – a combination of *Absolutely Fabulous* and an idealized beach scene in an ad for rum or chocolate. A far more satisfying way of filling your day than working for a living. We're sorry to burst the bubble, but the one thing you don't get in public relations and advertising is an easy life. They are two of the toughest, most competitive and demanding careers going, in which glamour is an element but hard work is constant. You would be pressed to find anything more highly charged and challenging.

PR and advertising are, in the main, separate careers but, despite their differences, they have many similarities. Both are used to inform and influence. They offer alternative ways of communicating key messages about an organization's image, aims, products or services.

Public relations is about communicating on behalf of an organization to a number of 'publics', ranging from customers to employees plus the media. As the late great founder of modern public relations, Edward L. Bernays, put it: 'The three main elements of public relations are practically as old as society: informing people, persuading people, or integrating with people.' Using communications tools ranging from the telephone to the latest technology, the one-to-one meeting or a special event or rally for thousands, public relations is about working with a set of techniques and applying them correctly to the task at hand, whether for a government or a brand of swimwear.

In advertising, the advertiser pays for media space to display its message. Advertising agencies create the advertisements that appear in the media. But, as this guide will show, there is far more to it than coming up with catchy slogans. It is a complex and sophisticated business, offering a variety of career paths, and it is hard to distil its substance into a few words. However, the Advertising Association offers one concise definition: 'Advertising presents the most persuasive possible selling message to the right prospects for the product or service at the lowest possible cost.'

In short, public relations and advertising are different ways of communicating messages. These messages are complementary rather than exclusive: a marketing campaign often features both advertising *and* PR. It is for the client to choose how much emphasis to place on each of these communications tools. She also has other options at her disposal, such as direct marketing or sales promotion. This range of communications tools is known as the 'marketing mix'.

A number of top PR companies are owned by advertising agencies or by large diversified marketing-services groups that also own agencies, while independent PR consultancies or in-house teams often work closely with ad agencies. Clients – who, after all, call the shots in any marketing campaign – expect the relationship between their marketing teams and agencies to flow smoothly. Put another way, they want their marketing to be integrated.

Some clients like to bring together the account handlers from their PR and advertising agencies to discuss strategy or tactics. The trade bodies representing individual professionals, consultancies and advertising agencies have also recognized the desirability of some integration. In 1994 they supported the launch of the Integrated Marketing Communications Initiative (IMCI), an ongoing attempt to promote improved understanding and co-operation between PR consultancies and advertising agencies. With this in mind, it makes good sense to examine careers in PR and advertising in the same book.

Each chapter in this guide is interspersed with case studies of women talking candidly about their careers. Some are senior, others quite junior, but all offer some insight into the business and the role they play in it. They also give invaluable tips about how they got started and what they've done to build their careers. In many cases their achievements have been hard won: it takes real commitment to kick-start a career in such a competitive business. But their examples prove it can be done and we hope they will inspire you to do the same.

Research by MORI, the market research organization, in 1995 showed that PR and advertising were in the top five professions that most interest students. Despite their huge influence, the industries themselves are quite small compared to other professions, like medicine and law: an estimated 22,000 people work in PR, 7,500 in consultancies and 14,500 in-house; less than 20,000 people work for advertising agencies. The PR industry is reckoned to be worth over £1 billion, most of that being fees (as opposed to expenditure, which is higher in advertising). After the lean years of the early 1990s, total advertising expenditure in the UK in 1994 amounted to £10.17 billion, up 8.5 per cent in real terms over the previous year. Of this, £2.38 billion was spent by the top 100 advertisers alone. Also in 1994, twenty-five of the top thirty advertising agencies increased their billings (the value of the accounts they handle) over the previous year.

The increasing choice and fragmentation of media means that professionals working in PR and advertising have to be increasingly knowledgeable to keep abreast of the changes and choices: in media relations, a key aspect of PR, new technology is helping to monitor and reach over 50,000 journalists working in the UK on 600 TV programmes, 1,500 radio programmes, twenty-odd national newspapers and thousands of different magazines. There are hundreds of local papers and a multitude of cable and satellite TV channels and radio stations, which all need to be factored into a media campaign (even deciding which ones to exclude can take considerable time and knowledge). The scale of the media today means that advertisers are more heavily reliant on planning and buying skills than ever before. Did you know that in the UK over 10,000 publications carry advertising? (Or, to put it another way, *Cosmo* and over 9,999 others.) It has been estimated that in this country there are almost 300,000 advertising poster panels. And whereas in 1979 there were a mere nineteen commercial radio stations in the UK, there are now nearly 200.

The explosion in commercial radio stations is indicative of the relationship between advertising and the media. Advertising allows us to have far more media choice than we would if it didn't exist. To an extent, it drives the media. But, at the same time, advertisers and agencies have to stay in touch with what technology is doing to the media landscape, investigating new opportunities like the Internet and the potential for interactive advertising on cable television. Meanwhile, the development of digital broadcasting will herald a dramatic increase in the number of television and radio stations.

The power of public relations is often hidden: when the law was changed to allow Sunday trading, few outside Westminster understood that a massive campaign had been running between those opposed to the changes, 'Keep Sunday Special', and those in the specialist PR field of public affairs, campaigning on behalf of the 'Shopping Hours Reform Council'. It was the latter who ultimately convinced MPs to vote us the right to buy our knickers throughout the weekend.

For the moment, the best-known advertising campaigns are those that run on ITV and Channel 4. They are expensive: while £50,000 is considered quite respectable for a PR budget, £500,000 is a relatively modest amount for a national TV advertising campaign. But there is no doubt that, at its best, television advertising is powerful: some creative ideas run for years, insinuating themselves into our popular culture – look at the PG Tips chimps and the Andrex puppy. Others become memorable in a shorter space of time, such as the controversial high-energy anarchy of Tango or the suave Gallic idiosyncrasies of Papa and Nicole as they zoom along rustic roads in their Renault Clios.

This guide will give you a feeling for what careers in PR and advertising entail. It also contains details of the relevant courses and qualifications on offer, salary ranges, useful addresses, a glossary that sheds light on the jargon, and job hunting and interview tips – everything, in fact, that you need to know to make an informed career decision.

In chapter two we explain in detail what public relations is *really* about. Public relations is often misunderstood, or thought to be only about getting media coverage, but the skills required are varied. Chapter three looks at the different types of work available at every stage of the career ladder, from your first job to running your own PR consultancy or in-house department. In chapter four we take a look at six of the specialist PR areas in which you could find yourself, ranging from politics to travel and leisure.

Advertising can be divided into three main areas: advertising agencies, advertisers and the media. Chapter five explains the different jobs in advertising agencies and gives advice on how to get in and get on; chapter six examines who is responsible for advertising at client companies and outlines the opportunities for a career there; and in chapter seven we show how advertising media are bought and sold, and tell you what it takes to get a job with companies that do the buying or selling.

Both PR and advertising are fast-moving businesses: they are perpetually evolving to respond to changes in the way organizations wish to portray themselves and what they have to say, *and* to the channels through which these organizations choose to communicate.

Against this challenging backdrop, there are great opportunities for carving out a rewarding career in which success can come early. Many plum jobs are held by people in their twenties and thirties. Unlike banking, medicine, law and many other careers that have developed over hundreds of years, PR and advertising are products of the late twentieth century. They are young businesses and the people running them like to recognize youth, talent and enthusiasm.

To thrive, you must be able to adapt readily to changing circumstances. The outmoded concept of a job for life seems positively fossilized in this field. If job stability and security are high among your career selection criteria, you might be happier in another line of work. But good people are hard to find, and in PR and advertising you can rise quickly through the ranks. A great many careers in PR and advertising are built by moving from one employer to another. Or, indeed, from one kind of employer to another. For instance, someone beginning their career at an advertising agency may go on to work in a marketing role at a client company. There is also some crossover between journalists who go into PR and vice-versa. People who spend their time at agencies or consultancies rather than remaining in-house will find themselves working on many different kinds of business, which appeals to the intelligent and creative.

The glamour factor may be overstated, and although lavish functions and shoulder-rubbing experiences with celebrities do happen, developing a campaign or seeing the fruits of your labour after months of brainstorming can be the best buzz there is. On top of that, the pay is comparatively good.

PR and advertising are probably the most potent marketing weapons an organization has at its disposal. It takes talented people to use them effectively, and many of these talented people are women, who have used their wits, drive and determination to make a go of it and have found genuine career satisfaction. To borrow a slogan from one famous advertising campaign: 'It could be You'.

Chapter 2 / **What is PR?**

Public relations is all about communication. PR professionals create and convey images and messages on behalf of a company, organization or individual. They are often involved in deciding what those messages should be, and when and how to convey them. Public relations is both a straightforward and a complex profession, which involves everything from simple persuasion to skilled management. PR techniques range from gaining press coverage to writing and producing brochures or media kits, or organizing special events. Essentially PR is a management function, used to ensure that an organization's credibility, reputation and image are protected, projected and secured.

Unlike advertising which often aims for direct sales and buys media space to achieve this, public relations traditionally uses 'free' space in media to convey its messages (although increasingly it uses techniques such as advertorials and paid-for promotions as part of a campaign). PR results could vary from media coverage for a jazz–blues singer to a change in public perception and the law about a crucial issue such as abortion rights. PR covers everything from the latest fitness craze to whom you vote for. Get the right message to the right people and you have effective PR.

Here's the formal definition of PR, according to the Institute of Public Relations (IPR), Europe's largest professional trade organization, which is based in London and has over 5,000 members in the UK: 'Public relations is the planned and sustained effort to establish and maintain goodwill and mutual understanding between an organization and its public.' The most important word in that sentence is 'public'. We are all a 'public' of one kind or another, whether we are consumers of products, employees, shareholders, or members and customers of a company, organization, trade or professional association. We are the 'public' of the books we buy, the causes we support, the fashions we wear. Small wonder, then, that PR is often described as a 'people business'. More than any other skill, you need to be able to work with, be interested in and understand what motivates people.

PR is also about reputation and image: of a company, a country, an individual or an issue. Take, for example, The Body Shop, whose environmentally friendly image is universally understood by its public and the general public. This image has been achieved through 'planned' PR, created over a 'sustained' period of time, using a number of different PR techniques over the years. Like any other relationship, PR relationships with the different 'publics' involved take time to develop.

Networking

In order to 'establish and maintain goodwill and mutual understanding' with a 'public', PR professionals do one thing more than anything else: they network. Networking is about making contacts – among journalists or people in the company or organization in which you work – and, above all, it's about keeping up with your contacts. You can do this by phone, fax, post, e-mail or in person but it needs to be done regularly. If you can relate to someone personally, and show them that you understand not just what they do but who they are, they are likely to respond to what you are communicating to them. Even if they don't agree with you, having good contacts who know and trust you is the key to successful PR.

Descriptions of PR

The expression 'PR' is frowned upon by most serious professionals, because it is a diminutive of the full term 'Public Relations', and reduces the multiple roles of the profession into two flimsy-sounding initials. Also, there is no such person as a PR, only a PRO, which is an abbreviation of 'Press Officer'.

Here are some general descriptions of people who work in public relations:

- *Publicist.* A public-relations officer or publicity agent, most associated with media relations and getting press, TV or radio coverage. Doesn't really cover the consultancy and advisory sides of the job.
- *Press Officer.* Confusingly, she doesn't just deal with the press. This role can include media relations as much as it can public relations overall, and project management in particular.
- *PRO.* The PRO is usually a PR professional who works within an organization, rather than in a firm of PR consultants, but for simplicity we are using the term in this book as a general abbreviation.
- *Lobbyist.* A lobbyist traditionally works in politics or public affairs, which is PR relating mainly to government policy, and seeks to change political opinion and, ultimately, legislation on behalf of a particular interest. This could be environmental, pro-abortion, whatever. Lobbying is not aimed directly at the media.
- *Spin Doctor.* Generally used by the media to describe a political PR's job. Although it originates from the idea of 'spinning' a positive PR message, it is often associated with a negative, manipulative image. Political PR is one of the most cut-and-thrust kinds of PR, and the term 'spin doctor' is tainted by the scepticism which nowadays surrounds politics.
- *Spokesperson.* Or, to the unenlightened, 'spokesman'. This term is used generally by the press when they quote a PR representative speaking on behalf of their organization. As with most of the unofficial descriptions of PR, this one does not do justice to the full range of the job either.

Regardless of what you call PR, it is, first and foremost, a *discipline*, which requires training to the highest standards. Increasingly, employers are looking to hire people with experience and qualifications, and details about graduate placements and required qualifications are explained more in chapter nine.

In-house, Consultancy and Freelance PR

The majority of PR professionals still work 'in-house', that is, within a single company or organization. The size of a PR department can range from one person to several dozen in a large company. With cutbacks and cost-cutting across the industry, PR departments and budgets are often overstretched.

The main advantage of being in-house is that you get a more comprehensive idea of the organization for which you work, and that can count for more job satisfaction. According to Tracey Meaker, PR manager for Virgin Atlantic: 'I prefer a more focused approach to PR, and you only really get that in-house. Consultancies are always held a bit at arm's length.'

In-house PR departments work alongside all the other components of an organization, which range from accounts to personnel, and, depending on the nature of the business, on anything from design to manufacturing. Sometimes in-house PROs start in a different function for their company and work their way into PR. Finding out that PR is what you really want to do is often the best guarantee of success: it's not a business in which to be half-hearted.

One of the main disadvantages of being in-house is that you can be on call twenty-four hours a day. You are also directly in the firing line if a crisis blows up, as you will be expected to know everything about your organization and its history. In book publishing, the in-house publicity departments often handle enquiries about books published years before, as well as the new books they are trying to promote. PROs working in-house are paid by salary, and may receive bonuses and benefits such as healthcare, company cars, insurance and pensions.

PR consultancies offer a range of PR and marketing-related services to different clients. Anyone can set up a PR consultancy – unfortunately, there is no industry regulation at present, unlike travel agents or solicitors who have to be registered to do business.

The PR industry has trade associations: the Institute of Public Relations (IPR) for individuals and the Public Relations Consultants' Association (PRCA) for consultancies. Both have strict membership criteria and codes of conduct.

There are nearly 700 PR consultancies or agencies in the UK. Consultancy sizes vary enormously from the giant PR corporations like Burson-Marsteller, Hill and Knowlton, Shandwick and Fleishman-Hillard, who have international offices and worldwide staffs of thousands, to small one or two-person agencies. The big consultancies are often called after their founders or partners, like advertising agencies and law firms. Smaller consultancies often have 'catchy' names like 'Groovy PR', which try to convey their own PR message to potential clients.

Although some companies have an in-house department and also use consultancies on a project-by-project basis, smaller organizations such as film or TV production companies will use either a consultancy or freelance PRO for all their work. More often than not, a film or TV production will have either a consultancy or a freelance PR working for them.

According to Quentin Bell, head of the Quentin Bell Organization and Chairman of the Public Relations Consultants Association (PRCA): 'Consultancies attract a lot of the best people in PR. A consultancy brings objectivity to a client, and has to deliver results. That said, some of the best PR campaigns are a combination of in-house and consultancy working together.'

PR consultancies charge their clients in a number of ways: they may be on a 'retainer', which means a regular monthly payment in return for their services; or they may charge a one-off fee for a project. Expenses, such as travel and entertaining on behalf of a client, are billed and itemized separately.

Some elements of PR work are charged for in hourly rates, particularly PR or strategic consultancy. Consultancies often keep time sheets so that clients can know exactly where their money is being spent.

Some consultancies specialize in particular 'industry sectors' such as healthcare or new technology, but most do a bit of everything: for example, a computer client may want to launch on the stock market, which involves financial PR, and the next year they may do a promotion with a leading charity fronted by a well-known celebrity, which requires both a different approach and different media contacts. A consultancy has the resources to accommodate clients totally different from each other, from a sporting celebrity to a government information campaign, or a new film and a human-rights charity. In-house departments often find themselves hiring a consultancy when a project comes up which is outside their normal scope of activity.

Freelance PR

Some people prefer to be the PR equivalent of a temp and freelance either for in-house departments or PR consultancies. Freelances usually charge a day rate, which can range from £50 to £500, depending on the complexity of the work and skill required and the number of days for which they are engaged. Sometimes a freelance will work in-house at a consultancy or an organization for several months, but they will still be paid at freelance rates.

PR Techniques

There are certain basic techniques to PR. Here is a list of the main ones:
- Organizing events, launches, news conferences or photocalls.
- Writing, production and mailing of letters, brochures, newsletters, annual reports.
- Putting together schedules for publicity tours and events.
- Media relations: getting favourable media coverage.
- Getting celebrity or VIP endorsement of a product or issue.
- Acting as a spokeswoman.
- Writing and sending out news releases or media packs.

- Writing speeches for senior figures in an organization.
- Producing video material, from corporate videos to 'video news release' packages.
- Providing consultancy to senior management about what to expect from media.
- Gathering research relevant to an organization represented and any competition.
- Advising executives or clients about strategy.

PR Categories

The skill in PR is knowing which techniques to apply, and when and how to apply them. Deciding what to do will be partly determined by the work in which you are involved, or the industry sector. Many areas overlap with each other, so you should try to know something about each type of work. *Hollis*, the UK press and public relations annual, lists over seventy different consultancy specializations alone, ranging from animal health to oil and offshore PR, but the main types of work within each specialization are: media relations, consumer PR, corporate PR, sponsorship, strategic PR, crisis management, business-to-business PR, marketing PR, fund-raising, and personal PR.

Media Relations

Dealing with the media is an essential ingredient of PR. Some PR professionals run training courses for executives in how to do it, which include a series of 'practice' interviews for either TV, radio or newspapers and magazines.

Media relations is also about management of the huge volume of media available to any organization. Over 50,000 different journalists are listed in the media databases to which PROs can subscribe, and knowing the media is one of the most powerful tools in PR.

Consumer PR

Anything you can buy is a consumer product. Any activity aimed at the consumer of a product or service is consumer PR, and this includes everyday products, called 'Fast-moving Consumer Goods' (FMCGs), from shampoo to biscuits, consumer durables from cars to fridges and leisure products like records, books or holidays.

Consumer PR is also aimed at people who 'consume' services as well as products: a government drink-drive campaign or a health campaign aimed at getting people to stop smoking are both covered by consumer PR.

Corporate PR

Large corporations such as Shell, ICI, Coca-Cola and Walt Disney use PR to build and safeguard their overall corporate reputation.

One element of corporate PR is corporate identity. The *Cosmo* name is a perfect example of corporate identity: it reflects in look and style what the magazine *is*. If it suddenly changed its name to *Square* an entirely different image and message would be conveyed! Corporate PR involves visual images, such as logos (the Virgin logo is an example of a memorable corporate identity), and has to do with forming an overall impression of a company or organization that is accurate, memorable – and favourable.

Some corporate PR is more stylish and personalized than consumer PR and 'corporate hospitality' at Wimbledon or Ascot is one way of doing it: it's a way of getting the message across in pleasant, impressive surroundings with direct access for media or investors to the main corporate heads.

Sponsorship

Corporate logos are seen on everything from catwalks to football pitches and this is all part of sponsorship, a growing arm of the PR world which is closely linked to marketing and advertising.

The main purpose of sponsorship, in which a company or organization pays to associate itself with an event, campaign or other organization, and in return gets to display its corporate logos and messages, is to get value from *association* with something that conveys a good PR message. When Mars sponsored the London Marathon, it was the first time they had strayed from traditional advertising into PR territory. Because the event was such a success, and its image worked so well with the famous 'Work, Rest and Play' advertising line, the sponsorship provided excellent public relations for Mars.

Strategic PR

PR is not just about communicating other people's messages effectively; it is also about creating those messages, and advising people, from the chief executive of a company to the Prime Minister, on strategy. PR professionals need to think about what could happen next. For instance, could favourable media coverage turn against you? If so, what can you do to prevent that happening? Are employees feeling involved and included in the company? How can they be communicated with most effectively? Will a change in a particular law have a drastic effect on the fortunes of a company? If so, how can you try to reach the politicians to persuade them to think again? These questions and decisions are all part of Strategic PR.

Crisis Management

Increasingly, organizations need to know what to do in a crisis, whether it is a government being able to handle revelations of 'sleaze' among its own ministers, an athlete accused of taking drugs or a pop star of sexual harassment. A crisis can blow up at any time, and unless it is handled calmly and effectively, may have disastrous results: a career or a company can be lost in a moment. The key to good crisis management is information. In 1995 the government's hasty announcement of problems with some brands of the pill resulted in a scare which led to thousands of unwanted pregnancies in 1996. The key to good crisis management is planning for the possibility in the first place and quickly providing clear information if and when a crisis hits, whether to news-hungry journalists, shareholders, consumers or any other 'public'.

Sometimes a crisis can be averted through having a good PR operation which ensures that senior executives are advised about any issues that may be looming in the press or are about to erupt.

Business-to-Business PR

This category addresses one business 'public' to another, rather than corporate or consumer 'publics'. It includes those industries or businesses that primarily work and do business with other business and industries, rather than with the general consumer: accountants and corporate lawyers target other corporates for business; in manufacturing, certain heavy goods like machine components are produced and marketed entirely for other businesses.

Trade PR is another way of describing business-to-business PR, and a wide range of trade media are an important part of media relations in this area. *PR Week* is the trade journal for the PR business; *The Bookseller* and *Publishing News* are book publishing's trade journals. Virtually every branch of business has one or more trade publications, which can be a good way of targeting other business, in much the same way as consumer PR works with mainstream newspapers, magazines and media.

Marketing Public Relations

In the past McDonald's has bought more toys from the Disney Corporation than any other toy retailer for 'giveaway' promotions to their customers; that is 'Marketing Public Relations' or MPR, the latest PR sector, which takes the classic word-of-mouth approach of a PR campaign and combines it with a product-led promotion. Another instance of this occurs when particular products are featured in films or on TV: while this is not strictly advertising or marketing, it is PR because it sends a message about the product without directly selling it.

Another form of marketing PR is brand-building PR. In marketing, 'brand' is a familiar word, and perhaps the most important: whatever you are selling needs to be packaged and identified as a brand. As PR increasingly uses marketing techniques, the brand image of a company or organization becomes all-important. Brand-building PR is often about advising people on how to know what their brand is, and then taking the message out to the public.

Fund-raising

You can do PR without fund-raising but you can't do fund-raising without PR. Whether it is fund-raising for a charity, an education establishment or any organization, fund-raising requires exactly the same principles of building relationships, targeting and organizing strategy as PR. People will give money to an organization or cause in which they believe, but they need to be *aware* of the cause and what the money is needed for – particularly since with most fund-raising other than street collections, you return to your 'donors' more than once.

Internal Communications

Traditionally internal communications, or the handling of employee relationships within an organization, was done by Personnel or Human Resources departments. Today, though, PR has become a management function: PR departments are taking responsibility for communicating with a workforce, which can range from a handful of people in a small company to hundreds or thousands in large corporations.

Internal communications can mean motivating or training staff, informing them of bonus payments or general changes coming within their department or organization. While methods such as newsletters, staff parties and memos from senior managers are all part of internal communications, new technology is being used too. The evolution of the information superhighway means that soon it will be commonplace for top executives to communicate directly with employees using videophones fitted to personal computers on their desks.

Personal PR

Today it is not uncommon for actors, writers, pop stars, fashion designers and politicians to have their own PR professional. Celebrity or 'talent' PR is also part of entertainment PR, which includes generating publicity for new films, TV Shows, books, albums and tours.

Personal PR is not to be confused with personal management or agenting, which is a separate function: usually PROs do not negotiate fees on behalf of their clients but they do just about everything else, from putting together tour and publicity schedules to listening to a client's woes.

High Status Profession

PR now has a high status and the skills are recognized as essential to an organization's success. These days, the most likely person to be seen regularly accompanying the Prime Minister or Group Chief Executive in their chauffeur-driven car is their head of PR, not their accountant or lawyer. With so much riding on the role of a PR professional, attention to detail is vital at all times – but PR is too fast-paced ever to become boring!

Rita Bawden

Age : **27**
Job title : **Account manager**
Employer : **Harrison Carloss (Newcastle-under-Lyme).**
Salary : **£15,000 plus a car**
Academic qualifications : **HND in agrifood marketing; B.Tec. National Diploma in business studies**

'I am now a full-time account manager for Carlsberg Tetley, the brewery company, although I have worked on a variety of different accounts. I am responsible for the whole of the North of England from Cheshire to Newcastle-upon-Tyne and up to the Scottish borders.

'My daily work involves liaising with clients, press and different suppliers, in addition to writing press releases and arranging photocalls. Any brewery-related story that comes up is over to me to try to get across in the papers. A large part of my job is also to prepare new business proposals and generate ideas.

'My first job was as a sales rep for Beacon Radio, but then I moved into PR. I got this job through a recruitment agency. I enjoy the variety in my work. It's important to remember that however well written a press release or well organized an event, it doesn't guarantee success. There is a major element of luck in PR, and that can be difficult to explain to a client.

'You need good organizational skills, presentation skills and confidence to succeed in PR. You need to be adaptable and get on with a variety of different people and adjust to all sorts of situations. An ability to spot a good news story is invaluable.'

Greatest moment. 'Managing to persuade the BBC to do a live news broadcast from a children's museum to mark National Science Week.'

Tips for success. 'Be original and self-confident when applying for jobs – don't just mail a CV with a long, boring letter. Once you're in PR, attend as many functions as possible, and always keep a note of everyone you meet through the industry, particularly media contacts.'

Angela Lyttle

Age : **29**
Job title : **Campaigns and research officer**
Employer : **British Actor's Equity Association**
Salary : **£22–24,000**
Academic qualifications : **BA (Hons.) in economics and politics; diploma in French, German and secretarial studies**

'Equity is a trade union that represents 45,000 members who work in the entertainment industry, including actors, singers and comedians. My job combines research, public affairs, campaigns and press-office responsibilities. My work includes preparing and writing briefs and reports – for example, I drafted Equity's response to the Government's consultation paper on media ownership. At the other end of things, I try to find big names to appear at Equity events, like those we organize at political party conferences each year.

'My first job was as an assistant in a small PR agency in Soho. After a year I moved into television research, and then into public affairs as a researcher/lobbyist with a small agency. I saw my current job advertised in the *Guardian* and filled in a standard application form.

'Consumer PR is very different from public affairs. In both, however, the ability to formulate arguments and ideas – preferably original ones – is the most important skill. The level of responsibility at an early stage compared to other types of careers for graduates is attractive. In public affairs the issues at hand are serious and real but, as in most jobs, there are some repetitive tasks to do. The one job I used to dread in my first post in consumer PR was calling up news desks and journalists to ask, "Did you get our press release?"'

Tips for success. 'If you want to get into lobbying, try getting some experience working for an MP or MEP beforehand. Talk to someone who works in the business if you can.'

Gillian Smith

Age : **29**
Job title : **Marketing manager**
Employer : **STA Travel**
Salary : **£20–30,000**
Academic qualifications : **BA (Hons.) in communications studies**

'STA Travel is the only worldwide organization specializing in independent travel for students and the under-26s. There are three people in the marketing department – a marketing assistant, executive and manager. I got my job through a personal contact in the company, and have worked my way up in five years from marketing assistant to being part of the senior management team.

'Although my job has "marketing" in the title, it's a PR job: I respond to press queries, plan launches, and meet with key journalists to generate favourable coverage. On the marketing side I organize competitions and promotions, often jointly with other organizations like newspapers or magazines.

'I really enjoy working with different people all the time, and rise to the challenge of raising brand awareness of STA Travel through specifically targeted PR campaigns. Each mention of the company makes the job more rewarding. The perks include discounted flights and press trips abroad – not bad!

'In my job you need organization and communication skills, and the ability to adapt. You also need motivation: wanting the best and accepting nothing less than the best for your company definitely brings out the best results. If you enjoy a hectic job, always being busy and coping with sudden change, and you are lively, outgoing and a hard worker, then PR is for you. But the downside is never getting to the end of your "things to do" list, when unexpected new demands are made on your time.'

Greatest moment. 'Organizing a really well-attended workshop lunch for thirty journalists and getting fantastic coverage afterwards.'

Tips for success. 'To get yourself noticed offer to work on new business pitches with senior executives, even if it's just researching. Watch others and learn from them but always be yourself.'

Claire Haji

Age : **23**
Job title : **Public relations assistant**
Employer : **Guy's and St Thomas' Hospital Trust**
Salary : **£14,500**
Academic qualifications : **BA (Hons.) in classics**

'I always thought I would be a solicitor, and did a conversion course after leaving university. Then I realized that it just wasn't for me, and I spent six months talking to careers advisers in London and my home town of Cambridge before thinking I might be better suited to PR.

'I did some work experience with a small consultancy in London, and then applied for my current job, which was advertised in the *Guardian* – there were over a thousand applicants. At the interview I had to give a five-minute presentation on how I would handle the opening of a new cancer centre. It sounds daunting, but I was determined!

'In addition to handling telephone queries from the media, every day I monitor the national and local papers and trade press like *Nursing Times* and *Hospital Doctor* for relevant stories or issues that could affect us. I also help produce the monthly staff newspaper. I also write and commission design and production for leaflets – I've just finished one for our outpatients. I also organize monthly concerts for both patients and staff, and liaise with TV crews who want to film here. The main skill in this job is juggling – usually ten things at once!'

Greatest moment. 'As this is my first job it's a bit early to say, but I'm constantly glad that I chose PRs instead of the law.'

Tips for success. 'Work hard. Enthusiasm goes a long way. Definitely get work experience if you can, read *PR Week*, and above all, talk to as many different people in PR as possible, to get information and advice.'

Jennifer Cox

Age : **31**
Job title : **Publicity and promotions manager**
Employer : **Lonely Planet Travel Guides**
Salary : **Over £25,000**
Academic qualifications : **BA (Hons.) in English literature and media studies**

'I make sure everyone knows about the Lonely Planet guide books for independent travellers. Nothing is too much trouble if it gets the company suitable coverage. If a tourist gets shot in a country that we cover, the media need a quote and I have to supply it. I am also involved in anything from launching a new series of guides to writing the sleeve notes for the music CD of our television series.

'I worked for years in PR for the performing arts, but I set my heart on working for Lonely Planet and rang them on the off-chance that they had a job doing press and publicity. I raced around researching everything about publishing and book promotions so that I could present a PR strategy at my interview. I badgered them every month for a year until they hired me!

'You need to be a good listener and a quick thinker in PR; try and understand every other person's job – like a journalist's – to do yours better too. Apart from general communications skills, it's important to be able to write different styles of documents, from press releases to itineraries.

'I love to travel, and do a lot through my work, but it's not as glamorous as it sounds – after a while, all airports and hotels look the same. The main perk is really making progress and achieving something worthwhile. The downside is that work can take over your life, unless you plan pretty carefully.'

Greatest moment. 'I recognize that any success I have is part of working with a team.'

Tips for success. 'Think about why you want to work in PR: good publicists identify with and care about what they do. Don't be frightened to 'do your own thing' but don't be too proud to recognize that you can learn a lot from other people.'

Julie Taylor

Age : **31**
Job title : **Senior press officer**
Employer : **The National Magazine Company**
Salary : **£18–25,000**
Academic qualifications : **BA (Hons.) in English and theatre studies**

'My career in PR began after graduating when I applied to the Arts Council for a bursary to train in press and marketing with a number of leading arts organizations including the Royal Opera House. Following the one-year traineeship I moved to Opera

North as a press officer before going to London to become press officer for the Arts Council. Three years later I saw the advertisement in *PR Week* for my current job and moved to the National Magazine Company.

'I handle media relations for *Cosmopolitan*, *Country Living* and *Zest* magazines. I aim to get coverage for these titles and particular articles and features, in other media, ranging from newspapers to TV and radio. I work as part of a team of eight people including a director and four senior press officers who are responsible for the PR media campaigns for all National Magazine company titles: *Cosmopolitan*, *Country Living*, *Zest*, *Esquire*, *Company*, *Harpers & Queen*, *She*, *Good Housekeeping* and *House Beautiful*.

'A thorough understanding of and interest in the media – broadcast and print – is crucial for effective media relations. The ability to recognize a good news or feature story, and to have strong writing skills and good general knowledge are also vital. And diplomacy and tact are always essential in PR. Equally important is the ability to think clearly about the key messages you are trying to convey with each campaign, and the strength of character to say "No" when the occasion demands. This can be one of the most difficult aspects of the job.'

Tips for success. 'Gain some work experience in newspapers, magazines or radio. You need a clear understanding of a journalist's needs.'

Chapter 3 / **Working in PR**

PR work ranges from basic administration to the responsibilities of a top executive. Almost all levels of the job require good communication and writing skills, effective presentation, patience, planning, organization, efficiency, creativity and, last but not least, cheerful determination. Above all, it's a hugely competitive jungle!

People often think that getting publicity and working with the media is all there is to public relations, and that can be a large and high-profile part of the job. Nowadays media work is so specialized, and public relations so diverse a profession, that you can work in PR and never pick up the telephone to a journalist. Remember, the media is one way of reaching the 'publics' you are aiming for in PR – but isn't a 'public' itself. There are vast areas of activity – from employee communication newsletters to client relations – which have nothing to do with media.

What goes into the average day of a PRO? Well, perhaps the first rule is that there is no such thing as an average day. As you are often at the frontline of your company or organization, you are the first person who needs to react whether it's because of a problem or good news: if you are representing a pop band and they suddenly reach number 1 in the charts you will have a *lot* more work on your desk – and in PR nothing waits!

As we outlined in chapter two, PR includes just about anything and everything that involves writing, talking and *doing*. In this chapter we will look at three of the major aspects in PR:
- Writing for different 'publics'.
- Media relations and getting publicity.
- Organizing events.

These core activities are often interchangeable and the range of activities involved in a single PR project is tremendously varied. That's what makes it one of the most stimulating and exciting professions to be in. It's also why you need to be well informed in all areas of PR, able to learn quickly and to juggle several things at once.

PR Priorities

The difference between a PRO worth her weight in gold and the comic PRO of *Absolutely Fabulous* is simple: professionalism. The glamour of PR won't last beyond a single job unless you know all about the business. This checklist of questions may help you focus on the day-to-day priorities.

1. *Who* is your 'public'? (Who are you communicating with?)
2. *What* are you going to say to them? (The message is crucial.)
3. *Where* and *when* are you going to reach them? (Timing and planning.)
4. *Which* techniques will you use? (Is a photocall better than a briefing?)
5. *What* could go wrong? (PR is *always* unpredictable: can you cope?)
6. *How* did you do? (What have you learned for next time?)

All too often the *reasons* for doing good PR can get lost in the rush.

Writing for Different 'Publics'

A large part of public relations work involves writing. Here are some examples:
- Memo to your boss outlining your plans for a campaign.
- Work-in-progress report.
- Speech or newspaper article on behalf of your boss or client.
- Request for sponsorship from a major company.

- Annual report or leaflet.
- 'Pitch' letter to the media.
- Press/news release.
- Contents of a media kit or press pack.
- Film or video script.
- Employee newspaper.

Each task may be different, but some of the same techniques can be applied. Above all, you need to be *clear* and *concise*: the chances are that whoever is reading what you've written will be busy, so you need to get your message across quickly. You also need to reflect the *house style* or corporate identity of your company or organization: if you work for a blue-chip city firm, the language you use will be different from the style adopted for a company producing fashion-wear for adolescents. Finally, whatever you write must be *accurate*, and this often involves research. Make sure you allow enough time to get all the facts, write the copy, submit it for approval and then have it sent off for printing or delivered for publication.

Media Relations

Media relations is the aspect of PR which deals with the mass media: TV, radio and newspapers, plus major magazines, such as *Cosmopolitan*, and specialist publications.

Media relations is everything to do with working alongside the media, and that includes generating coverage, which is publicity. Any appearance on TV or radio, or interview in the press, or mentions of a person or company or subject that is being handled by a PRO is publicity, whereas the work involved in, say, writing a speech for a chairman is not publicity *until* that speech gets reported in the media.

Media relations used to be called press relations (from the days when there was no other form of mass media), which is why the job of press officer – or PRO – exists more widely than media officer.

Media Services and Directories

A number of PR services and directories are designed to help identify all the media outlets, and update you on their changes. The main ones (see also chapter twelve) are: *Benns Media Directories*; *PIMS International*; *Hollis Press and Public Relations Annual*; *Hollis Europe*; *PR Planner/PR Planner Europe*; *Willings Press Guide*; *Editors*; and *Two-Ten Communications*, whose services include an on-line media database, 'Targeter Gold', with every listed UK media contact available at the touch of a button for information or mailing purposes.

Working with Journalists

The techniques for dealing with journalists are straightforward: you either write to, telephone or meet them, or provide them with written or audio-visual material.
You need contact with journalists to:
- Give them information – about the company or organization, or a specific project.
- Persuade them to cover something in their article/programme/feature.
- Try to persuade them, in exceptional circumstances, *not* to cover something.
- Provide access to people, places or exclusive information.
- Keep in touch for the future.

Journalists and PRs: Enemies or Friends?
There is an old saying in PR that you are everyone's friend and everyone's enemy, because you are often caught between balancing conflicting loyalties of a client/employer and the prying eye of the media. Some people still think this is true, but we don't: Good public relations is about *telling the truth persuasively*. Although

there are definitely some bad eggs in PR who don't mind spinning a yarn to get more column inches, there are also some unscrupulous journalists: some tabloid newspapers print fabricated stories to sell more newspapers and, of course, some people in PR will help them.

Some older journalists are antagonistic towards PR: they may feel that news or feature ideas originated by PR people are less valid than old-fashioned 'scoops' discovered by investigative reporting methods. Today there is too much airtime, empty print space to fill and too few resources to warrant that approach, and PR is increasingly being seen as essential to the process of providing and understanding news, features and the media generally.

In fact, PR and journalism have a lot in common: journalism is addressing its own 'public', the reader, listener or viewer broadly called an 'audience'. In PR, you are trying to communicate with all or some of that audience to reach your own chosen 'public'. A large part of media relations is about providing information to journalists at the right time, in the right way, so that they can 'cover a story', perhaps by sending a TV crew to a news conference, writing an article or feature, or interviewing a spokesperson live on air in a studio. It sounds straightforward enough and, provided that you respect the right of a journalist to choose what they cover and they respect what you are doing, it can be.

Nevertheless, many people starting out in PR often feel nervous about approaching media people. Here are some tips about speaking to and dealing with journalists:

- When you speak to a journalist, you are speaking for your company, whose ambassador you are at that time. What you say and how you say it may be printed or quoted, so speak *clearly* and *carefully*.
- You need to know what a journalist wants from you, perhaps a quote, information, admission to an event, or what you want from them, a particular kind of coverage, or perhaps valuable information, such as the 'lead time' or notice they require of an idea before they finalize contents and publish or broadcast.
- When you speak to a journalist you are speaking to a *person*, not

only to the part of them working for a particular medium. You should be on your guard, but you should also enjoy the process of getting to know them – after all, you and your contact are on opposite sides of the same fence.

• Journalists, just like the rest of us, have good days and bad days. Use your common sense: if they sound uninterested or hassled, ask when would be a convenient time to call – you may have called them when they are on deadline or about to go on air, and it's worth noting that for the future.

• Your job is to inform them first and persuade them second. If you want them to write or cover something for you, you are trying to 'place' a story. Remember, they have the right to say no, even if you think they are wrong or worry that your boss will think you've failed. Be persuasive but trust your judgement: sometimes taking no for an answer is a strength, not a weakness.

Media Contacts

No one seriously expects you to know *every* media contact there is, which, in any case, would be impossible, given how quickly journalists tend to move around, as television and radio franchises are won and lost, and newspapers are gobbled up by other media moguls. Staff turnover happens increasingly throughout the workplace. To be any good at media relations you are expected to make as *many* media contacts as you can, and to stay in touch with them.

Here are some tips for establishing and making contacts:

• Keep a contact book or an alphabetical card index system by your telephone and make a note of the journalist's name, number and details, when they called and why.

• When you have the opportunity, keep in touch with that journalist, even if only to drop them a note saying that it was good to talk to them, and asking them to call you if they need any further information.

• Make it your business to get to know which journalists are most important to your line of business: if you are in fashion PR, you'll want to know all the fashion editors, as well as the TV producers

on chat shows and other outlets for models; if you work for a political party or cause, you will want to focus on the political editors and those journalists who commission the 'op-ed' (see p. 149) features opposite the editorial or 'leader' pages in the national newspapers.
- If you know you will be meeting a journalist – at a press function or other event, make sure you know all about their medium – if they are a newspaper journalist, read what they write and the publication generally; if they are in broadcast journalism, watch or listen to their programme. It's not just flattery – which undoubtedly helps – it's also common sense.

Non-media Contacts

Contacts in any specialist area of your PR job are essential, not just those in the media: for example, if you work in public affairs and lobbying, then contacts in the Government, Opposition, civil service and trade union movement will all be important. Like the media, each group has its own range of directories and reference sources. Getting to know people, and getting to understand how they work and *what makes them tick* is vital to successful public relations, where you have to understand a bit of everyone else's job to do your own.

Media Outlets

Good media relations is about identifying and targeting your media. So, you want TV or radio or Internet coverage. Fine ... but what kind? Choose between news and documentaries, chat shows, magazine programmes, which have a format involving different elements of live and recorded material, debates, phone-ins, not to mention dramas, which have potential to mention issues or feature products discreetly – known as 'product placement'. TV and radio are known collectively as broadcast media. The same range of potential exists with newspapers and magazines, collectively known as print media. The potential for coverage includes news, features, columns, articles, supplements and even the letters pages.

Pitching to the Media

When you want to inform the media about your company or client, so that they can publicize an event or product or launch, you 'pitch' to them. Generally speaking this means that you write to or telephone them. The main thing is to be as *personal* as possible. This is harder than it sounds, particularly when you may be trying to reach hundreds of different journalists, and you don't know any of them!

Pitching is not the same as providing basic PR information, such as press releases and media kits, to journalists.

Here are some tips for pitching to the media:

- Tell them succinctly why you are contacting them, what you have to promote and why you think that what you are saying is relevant to *them*. For example, if you are in travel and tourism PR and are representing a new hotel in Lanzarotte with special disabled facilities, you should include media with a special interest in the disabled in your pitch list. Make it clear right from the start when you speak to someone working on a programme for the disabled that you *know* they have a special interest in the disabled and tell them *why* you are contacting them.
- Make sure that journalists' names come from a reliable, updated source, such as *PR Planner*, *PIMS* or the on-line media database 'Targeter Gold': people move around quickly in the media and if you send something to the wrong person they will be suspicious of its contents. It's often worth telephoning the switchboards of key media offices to check through the names before you send them as job titles often change, even if the journalist is still working there.
- Generally speaking if you do not know the person you should write to them first when you are offering information or access which you are confident they will want: if Princess Diana asks you to handle her PR and place her first newspaper interview, you can

call *anyone* in the media and ask them outright. Sadly, not every PR project is as hot as an exclusive royal interview, so be polite and write first.

- If you are writing, you should follow up the letter with a call, and this may involve being passed on to someone else, who in turn will need writing to and calling again. Allow *plenty* of time for one media pitch. It can take several calls and letters over a period of days.
- Do not be over-friendly or personal if you don't know the journalist or, at least, only slightly. How would *you* feel if someone you didn't know well started cajoling you with first names in a letter?
- Finally, make sure you are confident that they are in the right medium for what you are pitching: if you cannot answer the question, you should think before contacting them.

Press Releases

The term 'press release' or 'news release' is probably the best-known of all PR terms. PROs involved in news-related industries issue them, public companies announce their half- and full-year results in news releases and publishers or agents make announcements if their authors or clients get nominated or shortlisted for or win major awards. A press or news release is a piece of news information, which is sent to the press and electronic and broadcast media, often directly from a computer by modem.

Every press office or PR agency has a constant stream of information that needs to be conveyed to the media, but it is surprising how rarely this information actually warrants sending out a press release. It is up to PR professionals to devise other ways of communicating with the media so that a press release landing on their desk or at the fax in-tray is taken seriously.

A press release is designed to achieve three things:

- It is similar to a pitch letter in that it must answer the basic questions a journalist needs to ask, known as the four Ws: *who*, *what*, *where*, and *when*? News journalists receive hundreds of press releases each day, of which the majority do not explain in clear detail *who* is being represented; *what* is being announced/launched/opened/published; and *where* and *when* this is happening.

There is a fifth W: *Why*. Why is this news? Why should we cover it? The news release needs to be catchy enough and about something significant enough to answer this question.

- It needs to be *usable* in print or if read out on air. Information provided by a PR should be helpful and time-saving. The way it is written must be punchy and concise, and with a quote, or 'soundbite', from a relevant person.
- It *must* be accurate: the chances are that if the only information on an important subject is provided via a news/press release, the media will use it. Woe betide you if your fact-checking was wrong, or you failed to get the text agreed before you released it!

Press release format

The release should include the basic facts you wish to have and the following information:

- Letterhead or logo of the organization releasing the information.
- Date of the release – this can be headed 'for immediate release' or 'embargoed until . . .', but an embargo, which restricts journalists from using the information before a certain date, is not always secure and can be broken by media anxious to be first with the news.
- A title, like a newspaper headline.
- The name and number of the PR contact.
- The name and number of the spokesperson if different from the PR.
- The release should say 'Ends' to mark the end of the text.

An optional 'Notes for Editors' heading can come after 'Ends' to provide further non-essential but useful background information on the company or issue being featured in the main text. For instance, if the news release is about a major award, it should focus on the prize and judges, where and when it took place, the amount of prize money won and what the winner and their representatives said about the win – in other words, the *Who*, *What*, *Where*, *When* of journalists' criteria. 'Notes for Editors' will give additional information, such as the previous prizes won by the winner, any relevant sales figures, and other facts that may be useful for a journalist wishing to extend the story beyond news into features.

Media Kit

Producing a media kit or 'press pack' is another way of providing information to journalists, but with more variety and flexibility. Media kits are usually given or sent out at launches: it could be either a product or an initiative. Traditionally a kit contains information for both news *and* features angles.

The production of a media kit, ranging from commissioning photographs to writing copy, is a public relations duty. The following is a list of typical contents.

- Outer folder, printed or plastic to hold the contents
- News/press release
- Background statistics: 'Ten things you need to know about . . .'
- Biographical information on key spokespersons – may be brief or detailed
- Photograph of person, team, product or artwork of corporate logo
- Relevant previous press cuttings or favourable quotes to provide endorsement
- Copies of any relevant speeches given by key spokespersons or senior personnel

The media kit/press pack format is often used for other PR purposes than media relations, although no one has developed a different description for it. They may be prepared for:

- Clients or customers
- Shareholders or members of the board of directors

- Sales representatives
- Employees
- Potential new business clients.

Organizing an Event

Events may be an aspect of media relations, in the form of news conferences or photocalls, or they may be aimed directly at some other 'public', such as existing clients. The size and scale of an event can range from a small reception in an office, to a VIP visit to a site such as a factory, a huge political rally with TV cameras or a fund-raising dinner-dance.

Preparing for an event

There are some basic priorities to take into account before organizing an event:
- Make sure there is a good reason to do it!
- Make sure you have enough time to prepare.
- Remember that everyone should come away having enjoyed the event, understood why they were there and with a good impression of your company or organization.

Event Practicalities
- Find and liaise with a venue, including catering, security and staffing arrangements.
- Produce, mail and handle invitations and replies or advance information.
- Arrange for any audio-visual equipment, sometimes including exhibitions.
- Make sure that the corporate identity or company logo is prominently displayed.
- Compile a guest list.
- Provide press or media kits for guests.

- Produce an internal staffing rota: who is doing what and when.
- Arrange/handle publicity on the day/night.

News / Press Conference

As with news/press releases, a conference should only be held for *news*. This means that you must have a realistic sense of what will make journalists attend when countless others are held on the same day. Consider also whether holding a news conference will provide good pictures, for TV and press, and whether the information you are providing *has* to be conveyed in this way and not by another method, such as mailing media information.

Here are some basic tips for organizing a press conference:

- Send out a brief advance press release to announce that the conference is taking place. Target it well – make sure you send it to the right people – and ideally give at least a week's notice. Anything less than that has to be big news.
- Send out advance information to news desks and *follow it up*. You will need to check whether it is in the Forward Planning Diary, which most newsrooms keep so that they can decide what to cover.
- If you can, call in advance a newsroom you know and check that a competing event isn't already in the Forward Planning Diary.
- Make sure you choose an accessible venue, preferably a place that most journalists know and one which has reliable parking. It should have good audio-visual facilities, including power points for TV crews' equipment.
- Make sure the venue does not have an inappropriate name or connection with what you are organizing: there is no point in organizing a news conference to announce a new government package on disability allowance in a place that has no access for the disabled.
- On the day, provide media kits and press releases that give the main points of any speeches, including, where possible, copies of

speeches immediately after they have been delivered. Journalists who have to leave early to file their stories can then refer to this text.

Photocalls

Another word for photocall is 'photo-opportunity', and a photograph or TV pictures can be the ideal PR opportunity for media coverage. Next time you read the newspapers, look at the photographs. You would be surprised at how many have been set up as photocalls: new actors or actresses in a musical; the Prime Minister visiting a factory; a member of the Royal Family giving a prize.

Photocalls should, like news/press conferences, only be arranged for a reason and it is likely that the subject of the photocall will make either a newsworthy or sufficiently entertaining photograph. It is sometimes better to invite one or two specific photographers along to an event which you think might make a good photograph than to set up a photocall.

As with a news conference, you should send out advance information, both to news desks and picture desks, who work closely together.

The main things to bear in mind when organizing a photocall are:
- The weather: if you plan to have the local football team photographed with a visiting celebrity on the pitch, make sure you have an alternative if it's pouring with rain.
- What *story* will the photograph be telling? Are the right people going to be included in the picture? What will the caption read or the voiceover say?
- The background of the picture is important, especially if you are trying to include a corporate logo. The national press are notorious for trying to take the photograph they want rather than the one that benefits everyone. Sometimes you must be tough and not allow them to move the subjects around or change the background.

VIP visits

PR may mean turning the everyday business of a company or organization into a publicity opportunity with a VIP visit. Perhaps company executives from abroad come to visit headquarters, or the chairman/woman addresses the employees.

Tours and Schedules

Organizing a tour or schedule for a boss, company executive or client is often a core part of public-relations work, and it can be the most challenging. You could find yourself arranging a tour for a movie star in Britain to promote her latest movie, or a company chief executive visiting all the regional factories. Regardless of whether the purpose of the trip is to meet media for interviews and publicity, or different 'publics' such as employees, the basic principles are the same:
- Prepare a 'countdown schedule' from the day you start work on the trip, to 'Day 1', when it begins.
- Make sure that you list all the places you *have* to go to, as well as all the places you *want* to go to so that you can prioritize from there.
- All travel arrangements must be confirmed, but flexible where possible: if poor weather cancels a flight, when is the next one? If a train is late, or you get stuck in traffic, how will this affect the next appointment?
- Leave time for resting as well as working: an overtired client is never happy, and they are your responsibility during the trip.
- Prepare a schedule for the office and the family of the person for whom you are arranging the tour, with all relevant telephone and fax numbers, hotels where you will be staying etc.
- Make sure you know whether hotels are sending a bill to you or whether it needs to be settled on departure.

- Don't forget that tickets, passports, petty cash, etc., become *your* responsibility on a tour.

Fund-raising Dinners / Award Ceremonies

Charities and political parties are just two examples of organizations that hold fund-raising dinners, to raise both money and their profile. Often the job of running a dinner falls within the remit of the public relations department. Award ceremonies are common in the world of arts and entertainment (the Oscars are the most famous), but it certainly doesn't have a monopoly on them: they happen in business, the corporate sector, advertising and the public relations industry itself.

- You will have to book the speaker(s). Choose people who are high profile, but make sure that they really will be available on that date, before you publicize it on the tickets. At a fund-raising dinner, it is important that the guest speaker has some relevance to, or connection with the cause or organization, otherwise the publicity value is less and the event likely to appear more staged than natural.
- A fund-raising dinner often includes a raffle or auction. You must ask for and co-ordinate delivery of items, perhaps by writing to celebrities for donations. If the items are newsworthy or just quirky, this may be an opportunity to provide information to a newspaper.
- The event will need a brochure or programme, which often takes weeks to prepare, particularly if you want to include advertising and have to co-ordinate copy and artwork. It is your responsibility to make sure that deadlines are met.
- When choosing the number of courses in a menu, bear in mind the time taken to serve food, and choose food that you think will keep its flavour well if prepared in large quantities. Most big hotels and venues are used to catering for upwards of 100 people at a time, but it is often a good idea to go for a menu-tasting beforehand.

- Finally, if you are not happy, insist that things are changed: an event can flop miserably because details are overlooked. Make a checklist of everything you need to know – from how many coat-checkers there will be to the time of the band's sound-check. Then double-check everything!

Salary Ranges and Job Descriptions

Job titles vary considerably, but here is a guide to general titles and salary ranges in public relations:

In-house department	Consultancy	Salary range
PR Assistant	Account Executive	£10–15,000
PR / Press Officer	Account Officer / Press Officer	£15–22,000
PR Manager / Senior Press Officer	Senior Account Manager / Media Manager	£22–30,000
PR Director	Account Director / Consultancy Director	£30–43,000

The main qualifier for the job levels is experience: once you have handled a number of different types of PR – from a crisis to a successful media tour – you will probably be ready to specialize in the work or projects that interest you most and in which you have become particularly skilled.

PR Assistant / Account Executive

Despite the word 'executive', this is not a senior job, rather the first rung on the ladder. Most employers still ask for at least one or two years' relevant experience, but not always, particularly if you have done work experience.

PR assistants or account executives are expected to do a bit of everything, ranging from doubling up as receptionist in a small consultancy to answering the telephone in a busy in-house press office or communications department; faxing; filing; photocopying; taking minutes or records of meetings; and making tea. Background research is often the starting point for public relations work: it could be for a newsletter, a press release, or on a particular subject or the industry in which your company or client is involved.

Don't think that being in a junior position means you won't get out of the office or do some of the more glamorous parts of the job: you could find yourself dealing directly with senior executives, clients or media, first by telephone and then in person. PR can be a flexible profession if you are prepared to make the most of every opportunity: your department or company could be launching a new product or campaign and giving a party. You could be involved in putting together media kits with useful information for journalists, and find yourself staffing the desk where they collect them. The first person they will see is you, so you must always remember that you are representing your organization and be as prepared – and as helpful – as possible.

As PR is at the cutting edge of the communications age, and new technology is increasingly relied upon within the first few months, you may find yourself on a crash course in computers. Most bigger departments or consultancies run courses, but often you are shown the ropes and expected to get on. Job advertisements often ask for secretarial and/or word-processing skills, and it's always worth having some extra qualifications – they can make all the difference to whether you get the job.

Above all, this post is ideal for gaining invaluable experience. Make sure you watch others at work. How do they manage their workload? Who do they talk to on the phone, and what are they saying? This doesn't mean you have to become a spy, but don't be afraid to watch and learn from others – in PR, it's essential.

Lucy Renwick

Age : **24**
Job title : **PR executive**
Employer : **Northern Profile PR**
Salary : **£14,000**
Academic qualifications : **OND in business and finance; HND in business and marketing which included a year's work placement**

'Northern Profile is based in Newcastle and represents clients ranging from motor dealerships, house builders and solicitors to local radio, advertising agencies and fashion clients. I've just started to manage clients personally. At any one time I'm working my way through six monthly meeting reports for different clients which outline activity and diary dates, the work involved, media liaison, organizing photo-shoots and writing press releases.

'I left the Polytechnic determined to work in PR and began in a tiny agency in my home town in Northumberland, before hearing about the job at Northern Profile on the grapevine. I began on the reception/admin side of things, and am sure that my work experience counted for quick promotion to handling clients myself.

'PR is about getting on with people at all levels, and about juggling lots of things at once. With the media you have to strike the right balance – friendly but not pushy. Clients also need managing, and that's often the hard part. I love the variation in working for a consultancy, and how much you learn. But PR is also fickle and unpredictable: you can spend hours trying to get a story coverage to no avail, and for another client it just takes ten minutes to get fantastic interest.'

Greatest moment. 'Getting promoted quickly at Northern Profile and seeing my first press release in print – it was such a buzz!'

Tips for success. 'Get as much work experience as you can and learn to type – everyone should be able to rattle off their own copy. Make sure you research and prepare well before interviews or new client projects.'

Public Relations Officer (PRO) / Press Officer / Account Officer

For the sake of simplicity, we'll call this job the PRO. At this level you will find yourself handling your own clients or projects, and most employers therefore require a minimum of two or three years' experience. If you are working in-house, you may be responsible for a particular campaign, or media relations for a part of your company's activities, or for one entire aspect of public-relations work such as arranging exhibitions and hospitality events, or writing and producing the staff newsletter – no small task if you are in a large organization.

If you work for a consultancy you may look after five or six different client projects at any one time. You will need to know the industry of your client(s) in some detail, as well as their history. Generally you will report to a senior manager, and you may have some administrative or secretarial support. However, PR departments and consultancies are often stretched for staff so this may not happen and the workload will be heavy.

Depending on the nature of your organization and projects, the public relations officer/account manager's role ranges from being responsible for all of a particular area of business, perhaps media relations or internal communications. This means that putting the various PR techniques, such as arranging for the annual report to be produced, or setting up a string of interviews for a client and handling media queries, is all down to you.

Here is an advertisement placed by the National Autistic Society for a 'Press and Public Relations Officer':

> **We are looking for an experienced, dynamic and ambitious Press and Public Relations Officer to play a key role in the development of our corporate communications and public relations activities.**
>
> Reporting to the Director – Fund-raising and Communications, you will work closely with senior management in development (fund-raising), implementing and managing the Society's internal and external communications, enhancing and maintaining a positive image, profile and awareness of autism and the aims and objectives of the National Autistic Society.
>
> This is an excellent opportunity for a highly motivated self-starter who is able to produce first-class results under pressure. You will have three years' experience in a demanding public-relations role with substantial media contacts.
>
> **For this post we are able to offer a salary of between £18,825 and £19,689 plus London Weighting of £1,152.**

Ruth Reynolds

Age : **26**
Job title : **Senior account executive**
Employer : **Attenborough Associates**
Salary : **£15–18,000**
Academic qualifications : **Chartered Institute of Marketing's (CAM) Diploma, and a degree in sociology and economics**

'I've been in PR since I was 21. I got the job through a recruitment agency. I work with clients such as Colman's and Sara Lee, writing press material and taking press calls, and sending out client information.

'The job is very varied – no two days are the same. I find PR very challenging. There's no time to get bored! I would recommend PR, but on the downside it can often be very stressful, with long hours. Clients can be difficult and demanding. PR is actually quite an aggressive profession. Oh, and selling a story to a journalist is not always easy! The greatest reward is seeing a press cutting that you know is a result of your own hard work.

Greatest moment. 'Getting coverage on the *Six o'Clock News*, gained while working as part of a team.'

Tips for success. 'Be prepared to start at the bottom, often doing boring tasks for low pay – it will improve! It sounds a cliché, but hard work and determination to succeed is the key. Sending out speculative letters to potential employers got me my first jobs, and maintaining my sense of humour helped me keep them!'

Senior Press Officer / Senior Account Manager

When you reach this level, you will probably have more than five years' experience in PR and quite a lot of responsibility. Anything with 'senior' in its title generally means that you will oversee a number of other staff, and will have a day-to-day responsibility for handling major parts of an account or department on your own.

A senior account manager or senior press officer can be responsible for a particular type of PR work. If, for example, you work in a small consultancy that does a lot of public affairs and government work, you could find yourself in charge of all local government projects, and manage small teams assigned to handle elements of the work under your direction. Or if you work in a record company, you could find that while some artists get handled by press officers, you look after big names and star acts from abroad and act as spokesperson for them to the British media.

In a large organization or company, the senior press officer may also be chief spokesperson; you could find yourself regularly answering press calls, being quoted and possibly named in print or shown on camera as the source of that quote. Next time you see a news story on television, watch out for who is being interviewed:

is it the person to which the story relates, or is it the senior press officer speaking on their behalf?

Public-relations Director / Communications Director / Account Director / Consultancy Director

At director level, much of your work is strategic – devising, planning and advising on PR strategy at a senior level. Not all PRs with 'director' in their job title join the board of directors in their company, but once you get to that level you have considerable clout.

A public-relations or communications director, or their equivalent, will usually have at least six or seven years' experience, and will generally bring a specialized field of expertise to their organization: if you have been working in a local radio station for most of your career and have been responsible for a number of high-profile and successful campaigns, your next move could be to join a national radio station as their director of communications, or to join a large consultancy specializing in broadcast PR, and head their radio division.

At both senior manager and director level, you will undoubtedly be in control of substantial PR budgets, which may run into millions of pounds for large companies, particularly when advertising is included as part of the overall PR budget. You will have to show proven ability in managing smaller budgets on a number of different projects, so bear this in mind even in your first job: every time you manage a budget well, chances are it will be noticed and work in your favour for the future.

Jill Rennie

Age : **28**
Job title : **Associate director**
Employer : **Cohn & Wolfe**
Salary : **£25–35,000**
Academic qualifications : **MA (Hons.) in English literature**

'I'm responsible for a number of clients including Reebok UK, Whitbread and Motorola. I direct and manage the implementation of strategy and programmes. I liaise with clients, prepare new business proposals and manage a team. My job also includes media relations. I enjoy the involvement with a variety of industries and businesses and the opportunity to influence their success.

'I got my job through a recruitment agency, as I was moving from Scotland to London, and this was the most convenient way of contacting agencies. Before that I was an account manager at a consultancy in Edinburgh.

'PR draws a lot of women to the business and – wrongly – many people still view it as a "girly" industry. Certainly, PR offers a lot of opportunities for women to reach senior positions – often very quickly. You need good writing skills, organizational ability and a willingness to get stuck in and get your hands dirty! PR is a business which demands long hours, commitment, creativity and intelligence. It's also great fun.

'My job is very rewarding. Nothing beats the excitement of getting good quality media coverage for your client – it's still the most exciting part of the job.'

Greatest moment: 'Gaining the confidence and respect of clients who then ask advice and respect my opinions.'

Tips for success. 'Learn as much as you can from other people. Their experience may not help now, but will in the future. Don't rely on one success – you're only as good as your last piece of coverage, or project. Work hard and *enjoy* what you're doing. If you don't, you're in the wrong business!'

Michele Barrett

Age : **30**
Job title : **Media relations assistant**
Employer : **Shell UK Limited**
Salary : **Over £25,000**
Academic qualifications : **Three A levels and a diploma in economics**

'I have been employed by the major energy and chemicals Shell Group since leaving school, first working for the international company, and then for Shell UK. I joined as part of their A level intake of students, and it was when I was working in their information section, providing daily digests of news for senior managers, that I decided that I wanted to work in media relations.

'I handle anything from media queries to organizing media training for senior staff. We train them to handle interviews by practising with "real" journalists. It's my favourite bit of the job, briefing the journalists, as well as researching the best topics for interview, and organizing all the details.

'I also manage the departmental budget, and run our "Crisis Telephone Team", which is set up for an emergency such as an oil tanker explosion which could lead to a flood of media calls.

'There is a glamorous side to my job too: last year I was the go-between for a film company making a feature film with Sir Ian McKellan who wanted to film in our period building.

'You need to be well organized and calm in PR. I enjoy being part of a team, and I love the variety and unpredictability in the job.'

Greatest moment. 'I've organized several successful large live news conferences with TV crews and this year briefed a journalist writing a major 7,000-word piece on an issue of top importance.'

Tips for success. 'Keep developing your skills and learn to network, not just with the media, but with colleagues in the business and PR consultancies.'

Shelly Brett

Age : **39**
Job title : **PR Manager**
Employer : **Planet Hollywood London**
Salary : **£25–35,000**
Academic qualifications : **Eight O Levels, three A levels and is an SRN**

'Planet Hollywood is one of the busiest restaurants in Europe. My goal is to keep it in the public eye. We don't advertise, so PR is essential to maintain our high profile. We deal a lot with the film business, and I organize première parties, as well as promotions in the media offering Planet Hollywood prizes. A huge proportion of my day is spent on the phone. No two days are the same, which I enjoy.

'I actually trained as a state registered nurse, and made the transfer to public relations via the music business, having started managing a band as a hobby, which led to running my own promotions company. When I joined a PR agency after four years, one of the accounts was Planet Hollywood. Eventually I was offered the job in-house and accepted.

'PR is all about personality. It's about communications, whether verbal or written. You need to be sharp and able to assess situations quickly and not be afraid of making decisions. The hours are long: PR is definitely not a nine-to-five job, but I'm never bored; I never have time to be.

'There are lots of perks: I have been to the States twice this year and travelled to Europe three times – first class, staying in some of the best hotels in the world.'

Greatest moment. 'On the opening night of Planet Hollywood, when I saw three months of planning and hard work pay off – the event was a huge success.'

Tips for success. 'Decide which area of PR you would like to achieve in, research the companies, phone them and sell yourself!'

Chapter 4 / **Specialist PR**

There are scores of specialist PR fields, but in this chapter we will be summarizing the work involved in six of the more general areas in which you could find yourself working:
- Politics and Public Affairs
- Arts and Entertainment
- Fashion and Beauty
- Travel and Leisure
- Charity and 'Non-profit'
- Finance and the City

Politics

Who is the 'public' of a political party? The electorate at large, of course, but also its members, constituency parties, associated organizations, such as trade unions, and, given that politics is about government, every business, association, school, hospital or the armed forces. And, of course, the media.

Political public relations is not just about propaganda – direct messages aimed at winning votes or converting support from one party to another, most commonly seen in party political broadcasts.

Political public relations is generally sub-divided into groups that handle different elements: a team may be assigned to produce manifesto and policy documents; another will concentrate on media relations; and others on handling schedules for visits and accommodation.

Campaigns and Elections

Every time there is a local by-election or general election, not to mention specific campaigns on issues such as employment, a huge PR operation swings into action: the right cities and towns are targeted; speaking engagements arranged; the media alerted; daily news conferences set up; politicians mobilized to canvas; print production put in hand for leaflets, posters and direct mail.

Annual conferences

Every Autumn party conferences are a major opportunity for media coverage and communicating with the general public as well as internal communications with delegates and special-interest groups. A media room provides information such as the day's agenda, and issues media representatives with passes or 'accreditation'. Interview requests are constantly fielded, and copies of key speeches prepared and handed out.

Fund-raising and Membership

Fund-raising is linked to the overall public-relations activity of a political party: if the party is popular, getting good media coverage and most people are happy with policy, the membership rates rise and funds flow in. After Tony Blair's election as leader of the Labour Party in 1994, party membership increased by 100,000 – that is, by 30 per cent.

Individual Publicity

Senior politicians such as a party leader or cabinet/shadow cabinet minister often have their own press officers, who arrange their media interviews and effectively co-ordinate some of the most important messages about the party and its stance on issues at particular times. They often give briefings to 'The Lobby', which is the group of political journalists who do not report on what is happening minute by minute in Parliament itself, but on the latest rumour.

'The Lobby' is not to be confused with 'Lobbying'.

Central Government Information

Whichever political party is in power, the government of the day must have an effective public-relations operation to communicate its policies and services. Occasions such as the state opening of Parliament or foreign summits all involve the extensive liaison, organization, production and management skills of PR, as do campaigns on road safety or Aids and are all the responsibility of the government.

Local Government

Providing information about parks, museums and shopping centres, or handling crisis communications when a local authority scandal breaks or a notorious crime is committed, is all part of local government public relations. The scale of a PR job in local government is not to be underestimated and often commands extremely high salaries (such as £60,000 a year to be head of PR in troubled Hackney).

Claire Cranton

Age : **27**
Job title : **Reception officer**
Employer : **Metropolitan Police Service**
Salary : **Over £16,000**
Academic qualifications : **BA (Hons.) in film and English**

'Before joining the MPS I worked as a research consultant for an industrial research company. I then applied to the Civil Service Recruitment Centre and when they offered me a job at New Scotland Yard, I jumped at it.

'My job is to organize and arrange visits and attachments to the MPS for visiting officers, government officials and dignitaries, and I liaise directly through the Home Office and Foreign Office to set these up. I also manage the public relations enquiries desk, which receives 900 calls per month on anything and everything! I also help run the many press conferences held at New Scotland Yard, and am the liaison officer for *The Bill* so I'm regularly meeting with scriptwriters on the show.

'Adaptability more than anything else is essential for this job: no matter how well prepared, you can never anticipate everything, and PR is about not being thrown by the unexpected: I once had to arrange for senior visiting officials from a Muslim country to pray during a break in the programme at New Scotland Yard – but first I had to find out which part of the building faced Mecca!

'The main perk in my job is the sheer number and range of people I get to meet. What I don't like is that people automatically assume I'm actually a police officer, and start telling me about their speeding fines, which can be extremely dull!'

Greatest moment. 'Although there is a glamorous side to my job, I found an afternoon I organized for children with behavioural difficulties much more rewarding and memorable.'

Tips for success. 'Whatever you're doing, prepare and plan. Have a clear focus and know your audience – after that it's easy.'

Public Affairs

Ironically, public affairs is probably the most private of all public-relations activity, because it involves dealing discreetly with sensitive political information. It is also known as lobbying or government affairs. Specialist consultancies or individuals lobby for or against a certain issue or piece of legislation (such as lowering the age of homosexual consent) and have to get as much advance information about legislation, and who are the key decision-makers, before putting their case to them. At party political conferences, campaigning organizations take exhibition space or hold receptions for politicians. Throughout the year, activity heightens depending on whether a particular issue is being given a first or second reading or a Green or a White paper is expected.

In public affairs a victory can mean getting a tiny change in wording made to a piece of legislation, or knowing which MP, MEP or peer to approach to help your cause.

Arts and Entertainment

This typically includes theatre and the performing arts, visual art and exhibitions, TV, film and radio (or broadcast PR); and book and magazine publishing.

The principal kinds of work include organizing launches, award ceremonies and openings, arranging for reviews or review coverage and previews (advance viewings of a show for critics) and extensive media liaison, including interviews and features in the press, publicity tours and personal publicity for artists, actors, writers, directors, musicians or performers.

Another device is to put together promotions with newspapers, magazines or radio programmes, using the 'giveaway': free copies of a new book, video or tickets to a new production. This type of publicity is also an example of marketing public relations or MPR, a hybrid of the traditional PR endorsement/exposure in the media, with an emphasis on the product itself from the marketing side.

A key medium for arts and entertainment PR is the listings column: the section in every newspaper, and city-based magazines like London's *Time Out* and Edinburgh's *The List*, which feature forthcoming attractions and events.

Performing and Visual Arts

A new play, concert or dance performance, from seasonal panto to the Royal Festival Hall's latest concert or a new art exhibition, needs public relations, not least in terms of publicizing a forthcoming production. London's West End theatre companies tend to hire freelance publicists to promote a new show, whereas bigger, more established companies, like the Royal Shakespeare Company, have small in-house departments.

Performing arts public relations includes liaising with patrons or donors who subsidize government or lottery funding, and this can include fixing up a preview performance with a party afterwards. With live performance the need for crisis management can arise suddenly: when the comic actor Stephen Fry had a nervous breakdown and walked out of a play, leaving an angry writer and producer and disappointed theatre-goers, crisis PR was required both for the production and for Stephen Fry.

Film, TV and Radio

Often dubbed Broadcast PR, the PRO appointed to handle publicity for an ongoing TV or film production is called a 'unit publicist' and is responsible for keeping journalists away from the set as much as inviting selected media to it. She may also need to provide still photographs of key actors or scenes in advance of the release ('stills'), particularly to the trade media such as *Broadcast*, *Screen International* or *Première*. Before a programme is released, a preview screening may be held or, in the case of TV, advance VHS cassettes will be sent to reviewers.

Book and Magazine Publishing

Publishing PR ranges from a high level of media relations together with event and tour-schedule organization, from securing review coverage in books' pages to awards ceremonies like the Booker Prize, plus publicity tours for authors, bookshop readings and signing sessions and related promotional activity.

Publishing is not as glamorous a business as people imagine: alongside every soap star promoting their latest book of Christmas jokes or celebrity with their autobiography are thousands of authors who are little known but passionate about their book – and relying on the PRO to communicate it to the world. Competition for attention to books is intense, in newspapers or bookshops. Book PR is about aiming your efforts equally at five different groups of people: the author, the publisher and their sales team, the bookseller, the media and, of course, the reader. One way of publicizing a new magazine or book is to provide a 'taster', or extract, in another publication. This is generally negotiated by a literary agent rather than a PRO.

Magazine publishing PR is also about the cult of personality, of the magazine itself and sometimes its editor (and sometimes both). In each issue there are particular articles, features or photographs that can be used in other print or broadcast media.

Fashion and Beauty

The world of supermodels and paparazzi is certainly glamorous, and fashion and beauty PR generally has more than its fair share of parties, launches and free samples. That said, there is no less hard work or ingenuity required for the job. The fashion and beauty business is highly competitive, and very big business. The crossover between advertising and PR is more evident in this area than in others. PROs entrusted to publicize a brand of make-up, a range of clothing or hair gel, are often competing with major advertising budgets and PR campaigns from rival brands.

Fashion and beauty PR may encompass launches and receptions, in-store displays, catwalk fashion shows, or photo-sessions and fashion shoots. It is a product-led world, but also personality-led too: models are now as highly visible as the clothes they put on, and Kate Moss wearing a product or attending a launch can be perfect publicity. A well-known actress who says she uses a certain moisturizer or foundation will also boost the profile and sales of that product.

Even when disaster happens, fashion is so high profile that it can be good publicity: when Naomi Campbell fell over in her platform shoes during a Vivienne Westwood catwalk show, the pictures made the front pages of every national newspaper in Britain and plenty around the world. Advertising couldn't buy that kind of exposure.

A perfect example of excellent fashion PR can be seen in the case of Levante hosiery, and a launch campaign run by Gabrielle Mason Pearson from the Kent-based PR consultancy GMP. The campaign won the Institute of Public Relations (IPR) Home Counties South PR Means Business Awards. The campaign is abridged from the *Journal of the Institute of Public Relations*

Levante Hosiery, a top Italian producer, was unknown in Britain at the beginning of 1994. It makes high-quality tights, stockings, hold-ups, thigh-highs and knee-highs. GMP Public Relations were given a three-fold objective: to introduce the name, image and key points of difference of the brand to the UK trade to establish distribution; to build trade confidence and demonstrate continuing PR and advertising support for the brand; and to introduce it to the consumer, building loyalty through sampling.

GMP chose to launch the brand to the trade at the Premier

Collections Exhibition in Birmingham, one of the main trade fashion events of the year. The trade press reported favourably, and buyers became interested in the new company. The following month, during Hosiery Week when manufacturers open their London showrooms to introduce new styles for the coming season, GMP arranged for Levante to exhibit its style at a hotel close to the showrooms. This both took advantage of buyers' visits, and also interested the consumer fashion press.

A sampling promotion was set up in the *Sunday Express*, establishing immediate awareness and creating confidence within the trade. GMP arranged for the Levante stockings pack to be overprinted with the *Sunday Express* logo, and, in return for 15,000 free samples, the paper purchased 130,000 pairs to offer to each female reader. This secured TV coverage for the promotion in all TV regions plus radio coverage, and massive coverage and promotion by the *Sunday Express* itself. Copies of the *Express* were sent to all trade buyers to boost their confidence, and as a result the brand was immediately taken into major department stores.

GMP made personal visits to all top women's magazines to introduce the range to fashion editors and assistants, and samples were provided for fashion shoots and features. GMP conducted ring-rounds to the fashion departments to ensure that Levante was considered for forthcoming features. In addition, the magazines' promotions departments were contacted to set up sampling offers and promotions.

GMP also relied on the 'word of mouth' form of PR that is often so effective: GMP invited magazine advertisement and promotion managers to a suitable fashion event to talk about progress with Levante, and then asked them to recommend the brand to fashion assistants and subs who edit the pages. The 'internal' communication within the magazines proved successful, and complemented GMP's direct contact with the fashion editors.

The combination of the trade and consumer initiatives outlined here, plus in-store training on key accounts for hosiery department staff, in-store promotions and fashion shows, all contributed to a visible and effective campaign.

Paula Karaiskos

Age : **29**
Job title : **Press officer**
Employer : **Storm Model Management**
Salary : **£20–40,000**
Academic qualifications : **HND in fashion journalism**

'Storm handles over 200 top models including Elle Macpherson, Kate Moss, Dani Behr and Amanda de Cadenet as well as having celebrity, sports and acting divisions. I organize all the media for the models, as well as working with a team putting together fashion competitions around Britain during the year. Our last competition attracted over 5,000 entries, and we were co-ordinating over 144 finalists in twelve different cities.

'The main part of my job is media relations – representing models and celebrities to TV, newspapers, magazines and radio, constantly. But I also deal a lot with the general public, through the competitions, and also boys and girls who walk in off the street and want to be models.

'I always wanted to work in fashion, and started applying to companies when I was still at college, and when I left I did styling jobs with magazines. I got my first job in PR with the fashion store Hyper Hyper in London's Kensington. I was there for a year and a half before I saw the job at Storm advertised in the *Guardian*. I never thought I'd get it!

'In PR you need to be patient, polite, calm, and a good telephone manner is essential – after all, it's usually the first point of contact with a journalist.

'I love the perks in this job – I get invitations to film premières, and am entitled to discounts in shops and top hotels. Also, as Storm is half owned by Virgin, I get discounts on flights around the world.'

Greatest moment. 'Getting Storm a high profile generally.'

Tips for success. 'Read industry publications like *The Diary* and

Fashion Monitor and then write to as many companies as possible and try for a work placement.'

Travel and Leisure

This category covers everything from where to take your holidays to sports. The publics being addressed are both general and specialist: fans of a particular sport or holiday destination need to be approached in a different way from people being introduced to something for the first time. PROs for the travel industry liaise with everyone from holiday insurance brokers to motoring organizations. In the leisure world, the operation covers product or equipment manufacturers. Trade associations, like the Association of British Travel Agents (ABTA), or the Sports Council, who both regulate and provide information on each industry, run their own public-relations activity, ranging from leaflets to awareness campaigns.

The leisure world ranges from snorkelling to stamp collecting, and there are thousands of different publications and specialist programmes which all need to be targeted. There is often an annual calendar of events particular to an activity, and PR campaigns must reflect this: it is no good trying to get a feature on the houses rented by Wimbledon tennis stars at Christmas, neither is there much point in announcing a major new brand of football clothing when the season has just ended.

In leisure-product PR, product placement or endorsement is especially important: if a member of the Royal Family or a celebrity is seen suddenly to take up a certain pursuit, it will become the subject of media speculation and features. Alternatively, if an activity suffers from disaster – the death of a racing driver or boxer, for instance – this spells trouble for the PRO, who often needs to move into crisis management rather than pursuing general promotion.

Sponsorship is a key area of public relations in this field: having your product seen at the right kind of sporting event can provide excellent publicity, and many PR consultancies specialize in matching up the right product – clothing, alcohol or finance, for example – with the appropriate event.

Travel public relations not only handles destination in the UK and abroad, but also different hotels and venues, and methods of transport: the PR battle for cross-Channel ferries intensified in the mid-1990s with the long-awaited arrival of the Channel Tunnel. Airlines regularly battle for customers, using public relations to spread the word about the latest reclining seat or limousine service. While advertising is also heavily used in travel, PR promotions, arranged with newspapers and magazines to win free trips, are also a highly effective way of generating coverage and interest.

The travel industry is highly competitive but also, in PR terms, uniquely advantaged: who could resist the chance to have an all-expenses-paid free trip to a sunny holiday resort, courtesy of an airline, tour operator, or the holiday destination itself? PROs working in the travel business have to arrange trips, advance information and follow-up, to ensure that a journalist taking a trip writes about it – and hopefully favourably. That means paying attention to every last detail of the trip: the island may be gorgeous, but make sure the food is good too!

Tracey Meaker

Age : **28**
Job title : **Corporate communications manager**
Employer : **Virgin Atlantic Airways**
Salary : **£35–40,000**
Academic qualifications : **Diploma in business studies; and the Henley Management Diploma**

'My day-to-day responsibilities range from directing internal employee communications programmes, to managing media relations in a crisis, organizing major events and new route or product launches, and planning communications strategy and

PR campaigns overall. I also act as spokesperson for the airline and give media interviews.

'I started my career as a management trainee at BAA plc, and then moved from Gatwick to Heathrow Airports, working in their busy PR departments. After a year as an account director with a PR and advertising consultancy, I then moved to Sea Containers as group communications manager.

'I enjoy the challenge of speaking to the world's media on a range of sensitive topics, and seeing the results of your efforts is highly rewarding.

'The pace of life and entrepreneurial culture at Virgin makes a public-relations role within the airline enormous fun, but the job is demanding in terms of workload, difficult hours and stress. One of the biggest rewards is seeing a change in audience perceptions through the efforts of public relations activity.'

Greatest moment. 'The time I was a duty press officer at Heathrow Airport when the Gulf War hostages returned to the UK in 1991. The flight returned to a throng of over 200 journalists from around the world. Their need for interviews had to be balanced with the operational requirements of the world's busiest international airport and the sensitivities of the hostages and their families: pure adrenaline and the occasional cup of tea kept me going for forty-eight hours!'

Tips for success. 'Keep yourself well briefed on industry and business issues and think laterally to stay one step ahead. Remain determined, yet flexible and open-minded, even when times get tough.'

Charity and 'Non-profit'

As with professional organizations such as trade associations, the charity and voluntary sector or 'non-profit' PR, involves liaison with members, donors or subscribers. This means that some of the work is inevitably linked to fund-raising. Charity work may also involve lobbying and public affairs.

This area, too, is highly competitive: the public are known to suffer from 'compassion fatigue', an excess of worthy causes to support. Guaranteed media coverage can be a real problem for charities, who often have less glamorous stories to offer the media than, say, arts and entertainment. It is one reason why they covet celebrity involvement in their fund-raising.

One way of raising the chances of news coverage is to use Video News Releases (VNRs): specially commissioned footage prepared by the charity or a VNR company, edited and sent to TV stations ready for use. Over-stretched TV companies with tight budgets often welcome well-researched stories and ready-made footage, although there is also some resistance to it.

An excellent example of non-profit PR is the study, reprinted here by kind permission of the Women's Royal Voluntary Service (WRVS), winner of the Institute of Public Relations (IPR) Sword of Excellence Awards in 1995 and abridged from their 'Making Someone's Day' campaign.

What does the Women's Royal Voluntary Service (WRVS) mean to you? The war, cups of tea, middle-aged ladies in sensible shoes and green uniforms? Just one in four young people know of us, let alone what we do. In fact, we are the largest voluntary service in the UK, one in ten of our members is a man and we constantly evolve to meet changing needs.

Making Someone's Day was our campaign to address WRVS' image. We aimed to use public relations to show it is possible to recruit young people, secure public sector care contracts and to attract public and private sector funding.

A basic communications network to control information in, out, up and down the service was established. External publicity had to be original, to differentiate us from numerous other charity initiatives, without alienating existing members or clashing with our determination not to seek short-term solutions to our problems.

- A new corporate identity was developed.
- We marketed the hundreds of WRVS services under three simple headings.

- A synchronized press relaunch of the new identity was held at a national and local level, using a survey.
- New posters and leaflets were produced and supplied to members for local display using two new slogans: one for recruitment, 'Make Someone's Day', and one for general corporate awareness, 'Simply Caring'.
- Visits were made to: The Home Office, Hospital Trust Managers, Local Authorities.

In order to mobilize our 'secret army' of volunteers without losing external PR opportunities we:

- Developed a single vision statement.
- Launched a new in-house paper – *WRVS Today* – detailing the way ahead. This arrived by special delivery five days before the relaunch.
- Held seven roadshows and Q&A sessions. Over 1,000 key members attended and took briefing packs to cascade information down.
- Distributed new badges and membership cards to all members.
- Involved volunteers in the press relaunch – quotes, case studies, photocalls.
- Circulated press coverage to all levels – morale is boosted if volunteers feel recognized.
- Circulated guidelines on use of the new identity to all offices.

Outcome/evaluation

Extensive national and local media coverage generated by our members had a total reach of almost 49 million. Following our campaign a Gallup survey revealed a massive jump in the number of young men and women who felt they or their generation would like to get involved in volunteering. Gallup noted, 'A very big jump following your campaign.'

Recruitment rose: one office alone received 400 approaches from potential volunteers. On funding, the Home Office increased our grant by £250,000 and agreed not to cut the next three years' funding. Four hospital contracts due to go were successfully renegotiated. Internally, circulation of the in-house paper went up by 3,000, with 300 congratulatory letters from members.

The judge's verdict was that this was a 'classic campaign'.

Dee Sullivan

Age : **36**
Job title : **Senior media officer**
Employer : **Trades Union Congress (TUC)**
Salary : **£28,800**
Academic qualifications : **BA (Hons.) in English and American literature**

'The TUC is the voice of people at work, and I'm responsible for communicating issues affecting them to the media. The TUC represents 6.9 million people in sixty-seven affiliated unions but it campaigns for fairness and minimum standards at work for all employees.

'In addition to establishing and maintaining strong relations with mainly news media and handling media queries, I also get involved in speech-writing and preparing question-and-answer briefings. I also organize media training for staff, teaching them to handle tough questions from the press, TV and radio.

'Before I decided to work in PR I taught English as a foreign language in Greece and London. Then I joined the charity Help the Aged as a PR assistant, and worked my way up the ranks before joining Christian Aid, heading their nine-strong media team. Then I saw an ad in the *Guardian* for this job and knew I really wanted it. I applied and got in after two tough interviews. I've always wanted to work for organizations I believe in.

'PR is often about dealing with complex issues and simplifying them for a general audience. In any media role you need a strong news sense, and also the traditional skills of being well briefed, well prepared, flexible and able to prioritize – and stay calm when things get hectic.

'I enjoy the buzz I get from working in an important organization on important issues, but the mental energy required can be draining. Exhaustion tends to hit at the end of a long week, and even then I'm on call to journalists following up stories to do with the TUC.'

Greatest moment. 'A campaign we launched about asthma caused at work. It reached a very wide audience through national and regional TV and radio, and through the types of media not usually associated with the TUC – consumer pages, health and women's magazines.

Tips for success. 'Be professional – and remember, women have to be even better than men to get the same opportunity. Keep your energy levels up!'

Finance and the City

Since the deregulation of the market in the 'Big Bang' of 1986, financial PR has become increasingly vital to companies wishing to sell shares and financial products directly to the public rather than through dealers and brokers at the Stock Exchange. Every high-street bank, building society, pension plan, unit trust or insurance company invariably has a public-relations consultancy on retainer. This is one area of PR that specialist consultancies dominate. Financial public relations is one of the most highly paid of all PR areas.

Financial PR is aimed at shareholders (who may be employees of the financial institution), institutional buyers and investment analysts, the general public and finance and city editors. Institutional shareholders are often large organizations with PR departments of their own: they are the focus of 'investor relations', an arm of financial public relations aimed at keeping investors informed, up-to-date and pleased with their investment.

Financial public relations ranges from administration-based tasks, such as preparing annual reports that must address different groups of shareholders equally well, to handling the PR for a flotation (a company 'going public' on the Stock Exchange), handling a hostile takeover bid, or coping with the result of issuing poor interim or preliminary results to the media and shareholders.

Under these circumstances, it is easy to see why financial PR can become crisis or 'issue' management: a lot depends on how events and results are communicated. As Anya Schiffrin, Amsterdam Bureau Chief of financial wire agency Dow Jones News Service, says: 'The information that we receive from financial PROs and put out on the wire will often have an immediate effect on a company's share price, so it is crucial that the information is accurate. I have seen share prices plunge when incorrect profit figures have been announced – and the truth always comes out in the end.'

The Stock Exchange itself is hedged about with rules and regulations about how to disclose financial information relating to listed companies. You cannot, for example, simply send out a news release. The preferred method of communication is by electronic message – straight into the computer. However, there are rules about the length of the 'header message' you can leave at the top of a financial announcement.

In financial PR, while you don't have to be good at maths, you do need to grasp the formal and complex information systems that provide information in and out of the Stock Exchange or other institutions. You also need the traditional public-relations quality of good instinct, as the market is notoriously volatile, and you must be able to gauge how long a problem will brew before it boils over.

Clare Parsons

Age : **38**
Job title : **Joint managing director/partner**
Employer : **Lansons Communications**
Salary : **Self-employed and her salary is therefore determined by profits**
Academic qualifications : **BA (Hons.) in comparative religion**

'Lansons Communications is an award-winning partnership which specializes in financial PR. Our latest awards include *PR*

Week's Consultancy of the Year and Best Business Campaign in 1995. Our clients include Bradford & Bingley Building Society, NatWest Life, Kleinwort Benson Investment Management and M&G.

'Having started out in marketing after graduation, I wanted to specialize in PR so I joined Dewe Rogerson, the leading financial PR consultancy and worked with them for several years. I wanted to see if I could do it alone, so, as a prelude to starting up on my own, I joined a new City agency. Within two years I set up Lansons Communications in 1989 with my partner and we have grown rapidly and now dominate our specialist area of financial PR. Our initial staff of three has grown to twenty-one, eighteen of whom are women.

'Our policy is to remain directly involved in account handling, while combining this with overall strategy and management of Lansons. Financial PR is all about understanding the marketplace, and knowing that you can be creative with products such as mortgages and pensions, just as you can in other specialist types of PR.

'Financial PR can be tremendous fun – it's far from stuffy! A high proportion of our work is planning campaigns and dealing with the media, but also we undertake more general "issue management" such as managing internal problems or staff cutbacks. Maintaining confidentiality is critical when dealing with financial matters.

'Some of the more general public relations skills of sociability and style also apply to financial PR, and you have to believe in what you're doing, or you won't do it as well.

Greatest moment. 'I always wanted to run a successful company that was a good place to work. We now want to run one of Britain's biggest PR companies!'

Tips for success. 'Build contacts. Aim high. Join useful groups – as a member of the Institute of Public Relations, as well as being in their City and Financial Group I've found it extremely rewarding.

Chapter 5 / **Advertising Agencies**

Advertising agencies create advertising. But it is a common misconception that most of the people who work in them spend their time making the ads we see on screen or in print. They do not. The creative department is only a small, though vital, part of an agency. A far larger number of people are employed as account handlers, whose job is to co-ordinate the work an agency does on behalf of its clients. Then there are planners with strategic skills, and those who help to turn the creative ideas into the finished advertising. Plus, of course, administration and support staff.

Some 'full service' ad agencies also have in-house media departments responsible for buying media space – the slots in the press and on TV, etc., where ads are run. This function is also carried out by specialist independent media-buying companies and is looked at in detail in our section on the media (see chapter seven).

Nearly all of the larger ad agencies are based in London – which means that most of the opportunities in advertising are in the capital. Other cities with more than a sprinkling of sizeable agencies include Edinburgh, Glasgow, Leeds and Manchester. In 1994 four of the top five regional agencies, in terms of revenue, were based in Manchester.

Despite its high profile and continual impact on our lives, advertising is not a big employer. The Institute of Practitioners in Advertising (IPA), the trade body that represents most of the UK's leading advertising agencies, estimates that its members employ about 12,000 staff, and in all there are probably fewer than 20,000 people working for ad agencies.

About thirty-five agencies operate an annual graduate-trainee programme, with seldom more than four or five vacancies per agency. They receive as many as 2,000 applications for the trainee posts, and can afford to be exceptionally choosy about whom they hire.

Most ad agencies do not take on trainee staff annually. They recruit whenever they need to, perhaps after picking up new business or replacing someone who has changed job. Breaking into the industry requires effort and determination. Not to mention talent.

But advertising can be a rewarding career. It remains a business where, if you have the skill and application, you can make your mark at an early age. It is a young industry – commercial television only began in this country just over forty years ago – and one where personality counts for a great deal. If you want proof of that just look at a list of the leading ad agencies: almost all are named after their founders.

Some of the top figures in advertising are revered throughout the industry for their creativity or commercial perspicacity. But no matter how brilliant they are, it is still the client who pays their wages and ultimately calls the shots. Agencies are paid either a flat fee or commission, worked out as a percentage of media costs. Advertising is a service business: without clients it wouldn't exist.

Finally, one essential tip: when talking to people in the industry never use the word 'advert'. It's a blatant giveaway that you are not *au fait* with their world. Other slip-ups may be forgiven or forgotten. Chances are that this blunder won't be. Those serious about advertising talk only of ads or advertisements!

Account Handling

Account handlers are the main point of contact between an advertising agency and its clients. They work in small teams, often on three or four separate accounts at a time. Their main task is to ensure that a client's business runs smoothly. An account handler is a facilitator. She is responsible for what the agency does for her clients and to her superiors at the agency for the creative and financial performance of her accounts. She is the hub around which whole advertising campaigns revolve and pulls all the resources of an advertising agency together so that her clients receive the best possible service.

Account handlers work closely with their clients to acquire a deep knowledge of their business objectives and the markets they aim to reach. Once the objectives of a campaign have been defined, an account handler (although often it is the planner) briefs the creative team, which begins to work on ideas. When creative solutions to a brief have been agreed, the account handler 'sells' them to the client. This often takes the form of a presentation, where the handler talks her client through the creative work, explaining why the agency thinks it is the best way to proceed. When the client has approved the creative solution, the account handler oversees the development and implementation of the campaign. This means dealing with the creative team, traffic (the department in an agency which processes the putting together and sending out of ads) and the media buyers. She also works closely with agency planners, particularly during the early stages of a campaign.

An account handler may also be involved in trying to win new business, frequently in competitive pitches against other agencies. Some agencies have small teams dedicated solely to winning new business, but at others it's down to the account-handling teams to pitch for new clients whose business they will work on if the pitch is successful. Every so often account handlers may have to work through the night to prepare for a big pitch.

Typically, an account-handling team will be headed up by an account director, who will have two or more account managers reporting to her. Account managers usually run the day-to-day aspects of an account and supervise a number of account executives. Good account handlers are a mixture of diplomat and tactician. They need to be aware of what advertising can and can't do for clients. They need good communication skills, must be adaptable, possessed of more than a modicum of initiative and skilled at gathering information and managing budgets.

Starting salaries are £11–15,000. Account executives with some experience may earn up to £20,000, account managers anywhere in the range £16–30,000, depending on the size of their agency and accounts, and account directors £25–55,000, again dependent on the size of the business they work on and their employer. Board/group account directors may earn £40–90,000.

Sophie Vincenzi

Age : **29**
Job title : **Account director**
Employer : **Publicis**
Salary : **£30,000**
Academic qualifications : **Three A levels in English, French and history**

'I'm the account director responsible for L'Oreal and Royal Doulton china. My job is to think first and foremost about what is best for the client in terms of strategy, servicing the client and creative work. And to coax the absolute best of that out of the agency team. I discuss what's happening on my accounts with my account managers and update the agency's managing partner on what's going on. If, for example, L'Oreal is doing a promotion I'll talk to the media people and discuss the media brief in terms of publications the client wants to be in, in which position, on what date, and give them details like the size of the ad, whether it's colour, etc.

'If we're doing new ads I'll write a brief for the creative team and maybe give them some samples to give them a feel for the product. Creative work generally takes between two and six weeks. So, if you're a good account handler, after a few days you'll go up and see how they're doing and whether they need anything.

'Once the creative director is happy with the results, and I feel it's worth selling, the work will be mocked up and shown to the client. If it's something major I'll go and present it to the client myself. If it's a routine job we may send it on a bike because that's more efficient. If we're doing a radio ad I may listen to a selection of actors' demo tapes – which the creatives have shortlisted – to pick the right voice. It's your job to know your client so you should understand what they're looking for. But at the end of the day it's their decision. I may also talk to the girl from traffic to find out the latest on the production of an ad.

'I'm responsible for making sure that we bill the client for our costs so I liaise with the accounts department as well. As account director I'm really the pivotal point – and there can be a hell of a lot going on in every direction. It's my job to co-ordinate everything, and you have to be a little sensitive to get other people at the agency to do things for you.

'You have to like working long hours and working late. And I honestly believe that we're paid to worry. It has to really matter to you that you don't let people down. I love the excitement of a new campaign and when we do a big presentation that goes down well.'

Planning

It is said that if the account handler is the client's friend then the planner is close to the consumer. While the account handler is concerned with making sure that the client is happy with the service it gets from the agency, planners concern themselves with strategic marketing and business problems. Their job is to work out the best way to advertise a client's products or services. To achieve this, they have to learn as much as possible about what their client is selling and the needs of its target market.

Planners are briefed by clients at an early stage. Their main function is to ensure that advertising is developed in a way that plays to the strengths of a product/service and takes into account the attitudes and behaviour of consumers. An important part of the job is organizing and interpreting qualitative and quantitative research. In the case of qualitative, which deals with impressions and qualities and is often quite subjective, this may involve observing the responses of a specially chosen group of consumers, a focus group, towards the product. Quantitative research, that is, large surveys, is looked at to find out more about the market: for example, out of a sample of 1,000 women under thirty-five, how many have tried ice cream brand X? Planners also get as much relevant information as they can from clients.

Once a planner has learnt all she needs to about a product and its consumers, both actual and potential, she draws up a brief for the creative team. It is her job to explain what image the product should convey and to whom it is being sold. In some cases, once the creatives have come up with the concept for an ad, a planner will carry out research to assess consumer reaction.

It is vital for a planner to have a good relationship with the creative department. She must make her briefings interesting and help the creative team whenever they need further information about a brand and its consumers. If a planner delivers a bad creative brief, the finished ad will probably be wide of the mark.

A lot of planners also analyse the impact made by the advertising campaign once it starts running. This is called 'tracking'. Planners track campaigns to see whether consumers in the target market are aware of the product and what it stands for. The results are used when planning the next campaign. Planners sometimes 'pre-test' advertisements among focus groups before they are published or broadcast. If the reaction is resoundingly negative, the ad may have to be amended or even scrapped.

You need intuition and sound judgement to become a good planner. The job involves a lot of research, so you'll need to be comfortable with figures and adept at applying the conclusions you have drawn to the campaign plan. You'll also need to be a good communicator.

Starting salaries are about £12–16,000; a mid-ranking planner with five or six years' experience will earn £30–40,000; a head of planning at a large agency may earn £50–90,000.

Lesley Murray

Age : **31**
Job title : **Associate planning director**
Employer : **D'Arcy Masius Benton & Bowles**
Salary : **£30–40,000**
Academic qualifications : **Diploma in Psychotherapy, a postgraduate diploma in Business French and a BA (Hons.) in French and English**

'The role of the planner is to be the voice of the consumer. When a client is briefing the agency a planner must remain as objective as possible, and is responsible for putting forward the consumers' point of view, from their shopping habits to their attitude towards the client's brand. Even if this means telling the client that the brand they know and love is not particularly liked by the consumer. Honesty is mandatory for planners.

'The first thing we do after taking the client's brief is to interrogate the product or service. In the case of the product I would visit the factory, talk to the workers, examine the product history, use the product, pull it apart, examine it and put it back together. Then we interrogate the consumer to find out who they are, what they're like and their relationship with the client's brand. I do this using desk research, such as market reports and quantitative data, and then by talking to consumers in focus groups. The latter is where groups of past, present and potential consumers discuss the brand in a controlled environment. Research helps us to get under the consumer's skin. You need to know how to read research. There's often a gap between consumer perception and reality. Mrs X may have stated that she buys All-Bran because she feels she ought to eat it. In reality, she probably buys Coco Pops. A skilled researcher will probe that out of a consumer.

'When I am armed with all this information, I distil out the key issues and put them into the agency's creative brief. The planner has ultimate responsibility for this, although the entire agency brand team is involved. The brief is probably the most important part of my job. A good, comprehensive brief with excellent consumer insight and a good "nugget" for the creatives to get their teeth into is incredibly important. The best ads come out of the best briefs.

'To be an excellent planner you have to really understand how consumers feel about themselves and the brands and services they use. You need good intuition and sound creative judgement. The best part of being a planner is when a campaign you have worked on causes an increase in sales and creates a buzz among consumers. Knowing that it was your thinking that gave the creatives the insight they needed to create that campaign is the biggest high you could wish for.'

Creative

A comparatively small number of people work on the creative side of the industry. Their job, quite simply, is to create advertising. Their ideas are turned into television commercials, print ads, posters, etc. Creatives usually work in teams of two. The copywriter specializes in words; the art director concentrates on the visuals. However, because they work as a tightly knit team, thrashing out ideas together, the distinction sometimes blurs with the copywriter having some input on the look of the ad and the art director having some say in the wording.

They are briefed by either an account planner or an account handler. It is essential that they follow the brief because it offers an insight into the nature of the product and the type of people it is aimed at. In other words, they have to grasp the tastes and motivations of the chosen audience and connect with them, which requires more than a little self-discipline. They are also expected to generate original ideas of a high standard and their work has to be approved by the agency's creative director before it is shown to a client.

A copywriter must be good with words, able to write persuasively and in a number of styles. She has to express ideas concisely and paraphrase difficult subjects. She should have an ear for dialogue, be well read and able to draw on cultural references from cinema, television, theatre and art. She should also be ad literate – knowledgeable about the way in which words and images are used in successful ads.

Copywriters have to do lots of rewriting to polish their prose or to adapt it to the needs of the creative director, planner, account team or client. Only the very talented create a string of well-known ads. Fay Weldon, Salman Rushdie and Peter Mayle are all former copywriters, respectively producing the catchy slogans 'Go to Work on an Egg', 'Irresist-a-bubble' and 'Nice one, Cyril'.

Art directors have generally done a graphics course. They are responsible for the appearance of the printed ad or TV commercial. They sketch illustrations known as roughs or storyboards. Once a rough is approved it is turned into a final but the art director rarely does this herself. She oversees the process and may commission cartoonists or artists, although some ad agencies employ art buyers to do this part of the job.

The larger ad agencies have in-house production departments employing typographers and designers who take the art director's idea, turn it into finished artwork and hand it to the director to check. In the case of TV commercials, the art director, with the TV producer, selects the director and production company by looking through showreels. She attends production meetings, has a say in choosing the location and, usually with the copywriter, will go on the shoot to supervise the filming. Art directors must also be ad literate.

Creatives have to cope with a lot of pressure. They have to come up with punchy, imaginative, memorable ads to tight deadlines. And these ads need to match the client's objectives, which could be anything from changing the image of a service to increasing sales of a product.

Far more people want to become creatives than ever make the grade. But if you think it's for you, you'll need to be determined and able to withstand no-holds-barred criticism of your work.

Having your ideas torn to pieces and unceremoniously rejected by seniors is part of the learning process.

The handful of creative leading lights are very well paid indeed: a few earn over £100,000 a year. But for those just starting the pay is dismal – there is so much competition for places that most are relieved just to get a foot on the ladder and will work for next to nothing. This is not a career that promises instant riches, but if you get in, and make your mark, agencies will pay you well. An established creative may earn about £30,000. Senior creatives at large agencies could be paid anywhere between £35 and £70,000, with creative directors on £50–100,000.

Rachel Carroll

Age : **30**
Job title : **Copywriter**
Employer : **Howell Henry Chaldecott Lury**
Salary : **£27,000**
Academic qualifications : **BA (Hons.) English**

'People think that copywriting is all about coming up with slogans but the basic thrust of the job is creating ideas and concepts. I work as a team with art director Yuval Zommer and we bounce ideas off each other. The account people work out what the strategy should be and we work out the creative solution. The reason I like my job is that it's just you and your brain facing a blank piece of paper or computer screen. It's down to me to find a different way of seeing things. I get a real kick when I get a good idea and put it down on paper.

'My job also involves choosing directors for and casting TV commercials, and helping produce radio ads. You have the opportunity to work with other creative people like directors and photographers – and I'd say I was out and about with Yuval doing that sort of thing 30 per cent of the time. I've got a complete antipathy to finding things in files and looking up figures, so for me copywriting is the best job in advertising. My job is to make the client fall in love with their product. But it can be depressing when you come up with a good idea and the client can't see it.

'I'm currently working on a project for the AA, which I'm afraid I can't talk about yet. My most famous campaign to date was for the English Collective of Prostitutes, which I did when I was at Bartle Bogle Hegarty. I was interested in breaking down the barriers between prostitutes and non-prostitutes at a time when prostitutes were being fined in court for carrying condoms. One of my ads said, "What do you call men who take money from prostitutes? Magistrates." I got a few awards for that, which was nice, but they're not really that important. The most important thing is that *you* think your work's good. It should have integrity, not phoney aspirations. It should tell people what the product is and put it in context in a charming way.'

Creative Services

The creative services department is an ad agency's engine room. Without it, press, poster and direct mail ads would never see the light of day. Quite simply, it services the creative work from the idea to the finished ad.

There are several different jobs within creative services, all linked to progressing or producing ads (mainly press and poster ads; television, cinema and radio ads are usually handled by a separate TV/broadcast department, if the agency has one). A decade ago, when print ad production still predominantly involved old-fashioned and somewhat grubby manual typesetting methods, it was a career dominated by men. But with the advent of new technology – in particular, on-screen design in the shape of the Apple Macintosh – it is an area that now attracts many women.

Most full service ad agencies have a creative services director who has overall responsibility for running the department, making sure it stays within its budgets and maintains quality standards. She oversees people doing traffic/production, art buying, print buying and working in the studio. At some smaller agencies some of these roles may be combined.

At most agencies the role of traffic is combined with production. Those in *traffic/production* ensure that everyone who is involved in the development and progress of an ad is fully informed at every stage. They see the ad through from start to finish. At the beginning of the ad production cycle, the traffic/production person talks to the account handlers to find out how much advertising their clients are likely to do in the near future. She notes this, keeps an eye on the situation and then chases up the account handlers for updates.

Once a job has been briefed to the account handlers by the client, it is traffic/production's responsibility to co-ordinate its progress. This entails keeping in regular contact with the copywriter and art director to monitor the status of the job. When the concept for the ad has been approved, the traffic/production person attends pre-production meetings where the time it will take to produce an ad and its production budget are agreed. It is then up to her to get the job distributed to various departments, for instance to the art buyers and the studio. She may deal directly with external illustrators or photographers, and must keep the account handlers, creatives and her departmental boss constantly informed of the job's progress – they may have to clear it at various stages – and report any problems. She makes sure that the finished ad appears as agreed by the agency and its client, and that production costs do not exceed the budget. It is down to her to supply the copy to the appropriate publications in the format they require. Deadlines can be tight, so you must respond well under pressure. You also need to build good working relationships with colleagues in other departments.

An *art buyer* negotiates with independent photographers and illustrators to get photographs and illustrations of the best quality at the lowest price. She consults with the art director, who frequently has strong views on the style of art required and may even have a particular photographer or illustrator in mind. Sometimes she has to reconcile what the creatives want with the limitations of the budget. Usually she will talk to a number of photographers or illustrators to get the most competitive quote.

She must keep in touch with leading photographers and illustrators but also search out new talent, which may involve getting to know about promising students at art colleges and attending end-of-year degree shows. She will look at the portfolios of photographers and artists who come to see her at the agency, and she will keep abreast of what's happening in magazines to see if they are using any innovative or technically accomplished new talent.

Although dealing with artists and photographers may sound glamorous, art buying is hard work. Art buyers seldom go on shoots: it is an office-based job. The qualities you need are a good artistic eye, canny negotiating skills and the ability to work well with your colleagues. Not all agencies employ specialist art buyers; in some cases the job is done by art directors, in others by someone filling a number of creative services roles.

The *print buyer* also needs strong negotiating skills. She buys the paper for direct mail campaigns, sales promotions and poster advertising. She needs to know about different qualities of paper, how they are affected by the printing process and must develop an extensive contact base among suppliers, plus a knowledge of the types of paper they stock.

The *studio* staff take the copywriter's words, art director's roughs and the original photography/illustrations and lay them out to make what is known as the finished artwork. The process involves several different skills. Some ad agency art studios employ specialist typographers (sometimes called type designers) whose job is to pick the most appropriate typefaces for a job. Another activity in the studio is retouching photographs to alter the image or improve their quality, although agencies without large in-house facilities may use an independent reproduction house for any retouching they need. Retouching can be done either manually or on screen after the image has been scanned into the computer.

The designers or Mac operators in the studio turn the concept rough plus any typographical instructions into the finished artwork. Most of this is now done on desktop computers, predominantly the Apple Macintosh. Studio staff also incorporate 'mechanical instructions', which explain how the ad is to be printed, into a job.

The finished artwork is often sent out on computer disk – and, increasingly, directly down an ISDN phone line – to the repro house where the separated films necessary for printing colour ads are produced. Film for black-and-white ads may be produced by the studio itself and may go directly from the ad agency to the publication in which it is to appear. Studio staff must be computer literate; experience of using an Apple Mac counts for a lot. A flair for design is essential. Every so often a studio junior vacancy comes up that doesn't require any art qualifications and offers some on-the-job training but these are few and far between. Most studio jobs go to those who have completed an art or design course.

Creative services first jobbers at small agencies may be paid as little as £6,000. Traffic/production assistants with some experience generally earn £10–16,000. Traffic/production controllers, senior studio staff and senior art buyers will earn over £20,000, while creative services directors get up to £50,000.

Lorna Brown

Age : **23**
Job title : **Traffic assistant**
Employer : **The Morgan Partnership**
Salary : **£11–13,000**
Academic qualifications : **Five O Levels including art**

'My career in advertising started directly out of school when I began a YTS at Barker's, Scotland. After a month I was taken on full time and began my training as a junior traffic assistant, learning the basics of how an advertising agency works. Barker's also sent me on the advertising course at the College of Commerce in

Glasgow, which had modules on art and design, media studies and PR.

'In the three advertising agencies where I have worked the traffic/production systems are similar although at the Morgan Partnership we are changing from a manually operated to a Mac-operated one.

'The traffic department's main responsibility is to oversee every job that enters the agency from start to completion. I'm briefed by the account handlers who get their briefs from the client. When a job is first briefed in, it's the traffic department's responsibility to distribute it to the appropriate departments, that is creative, studio, media. That involves briefing the creatives to do a layout or getting the studio to do finished artwork.

'We have to constantly check on progress as our deadlines are usually urgent. Every job must have a deadline, whether it be for press, radio or TV. The production side of it comes in later, once the job has been approved by account handler and client.

'When the job is at its final stage we find out what the requirements are, such as film for colour print ads, digital audiotapes for radio and videotape for TV. We arrange this with outside suppliers.

'Finally, it is also the department's responsibility to organize the safe despatch of this material. On the whole, traffic/production departments are probably what you could class as the heart of the agency. I'd thoroughly recommend it as a career – as long as you thrive on stress. I like to run about and check everything, making sure a job's on time and going okay. I enjoy being in the midst of everything.'

TV Department

The TV department is responsible for getting the television and radio commercials made. As the ads are nearly always made by specialist external production companies, TV departments tend to be small. They may employ only one or two full-time producers supported by a couple of PAs and TV secretaries.

An agency producer/head of TV's job begins when she liaises with the account handlers to find out when a job is likely to come through, then plans ahead to make sure there will be time to deal with it. She keeps up to date with the directors working in advertising – who may also work in films and television – and when a script comes through from the creative department she will draw up a shortlist of appropriate directors. She will then look at their showreels – probably with the creative team – and decide whom to commission.

Most directors are attached to independent production companies, which handle the details of arranging a shoot. But the ad agency producer keeps a watchful eye on things, making sure, for example, that the director has selected a cameraman with the right sort of experience and that production costs do not exceed the agreed budget. The producer will usually go along to the shoot with the creative team to make sure that it progresses smoothly. She deals with any problems that may crop up. It can be difficult to balance the occasionally conflicting needs of the creative team, the director and the advertiser. Sometimes long hours are necessary – a shoot may start at 8 a.m. and finish at 10 p.m. But there are compensations: a lot of commercials are shot overseas.

The PAs and secretaries in the TV department deal with the production details that producers don't have time to attend to. They may book the recording studio and voiceover actors for a radio ad. Once they have gained some experience they may accompany the creative team to the studio and produce the ad themselves. Beginning as a secretary/PA in the TV department is the best way to become an ad agency TV producer.

Starting salaries are about £12–15,000. Established producers may earn £25–30,000 and senior producers £50,000.

Film Production

Independent film production companies make TV commercials under the supervision of a commissioning advertising agency.

They work to a brief from the agency's TV producer to film a script written by the agency's creative team.

Film production companies usually have a number of directors on contract. When a director has been chosen by the agency the production company works alongside her to assemble the production team such as the camera operator and sound recordist. It is the production company's job to oversee the casting and shooting of the commercial on film or videotape, either in a studio or on location. It then supervises the cutting, editing, sound recording, mixing and so on.

Production companies employ producers to co-ordinate the process, of whom many have worked their way up from junior jobs such as PA/receptionist. The other way in is as a runner, who carries out errands, makes the tea and learns about the business by helping out on shoots. Many directors have started out as runners because the job offers the chance to see film-making at first hand. So if you're set on directing rather than producing, and haven't attended a film course, apply for jobs as a runner instead of as a PA.

These entry level jobs can be quite punishing, demanding long hours for low wages, but there is no shortage of takers because, for the talented, they offer the opportunity to become a producer or director. And the best in the business go on to expand their activities beyond advertising. Here's a brief list of some of the top British movie directors to have crossed over from making commercials: Alan Parker (*Midnight Express, The Commitments*), Ridley Scott (*Blade Runner, Thelma & Louise*), Tony Scott (*Top Gun, True Romance*), Adrian Lyne (*Fatal Attraction, Indecent Proposal*).

Helen Langridge

Age : **33**
Job title : **Owner**
Employer : **Helen Langridge Associates**
Salary : **£70,000**
Academic qualifications : **Three O Levels in art, English and history**

'I started out as a receptionist and set up in business on my own nine years ago. I love this business and the way it can go from being quiet one day to absolutely frantic the next. We have directors on contract with us but I'm always looking for new talent. I watch all the film students' graduate reels. And if I see something that makes me think they'll be a good commercials director I might try to sign them up. I work closely with our directors. It's part of my job to market them – I go out and show their stuff to agencies.

'When we're given a commercial to make I will guide a director through the script. The director handles the creative part, such as deciding on sets, while our job as the production company is to organize things and make it happen. We have to budget it – you get to know how much things cost. Sometimes a commercial will need three sets, sometimes we'll have to go on location. Perhaps we'll need an unusual crane that will add to the cost. If we need a shot I try to work out a way of getting it. It gives me a lot of pleasure to see directors we've worked with go on to be successful and do films. The things I'm most proud of are the jobs with young directors.

'In my job I've been able to see lots of the world. If you're shooting overseas and you've got a local person acting as your production manager you get to see places you wouldn't see if you were backpacking on your own. We've done commercials for Levi's, BT, Adidas, Nike with Eric Cantona, the Foster's Ice ski-jumping kangaroo, and I'm just working on one for Red Stripe with the director Spike Lee.

'I'd like to ask women coming into this business to think carefully about what they want to do. If they are in any way creative I'd urge them to give the creative side a shot. There are a lot of women producers but not nearly enough women directors.'

Getting in and Getting Ahead

As we've pointed out already, it is notoriously hard to get into advertising. It takes enthusiasm and determination in spades to persuade an agency to give you a chance. And there are far more people wanting to work in advertising than there are jobs available. But if you think it's what you want to do and that you've got what it takes to do it, then keep plugging away. Here are a few pointers that may shift the odds in your favour.

First and foremost, decide what you want out of a career in advertising and the type of work you want to do. Chances are that if you are applying for jobs as an account handler and a copywriter at the same time, you won't get very far. You need to be focused. Or – if you're not really sure but think you might like to try advertising as a career – at least appear focused to prospective employers.

Keep up to date with what's happening in the agency world. Read the trade press and make sure you have a fair idea of who's behind the larger current campaigns and what important bits of new business agencies have picked up. You should also make sure you have a reasonable idea of where agencies stand in the pecking order. The best source of information for this is the league table of the top 300 UK advertising agencies published every year by the trade publication *Campaign*.

Be thorough in your research. Find out who the agency's main clients are and something about its history. Is it a young agency? Was it created out of a merger? Is it publicly or privately owned? Is it a subsidiary of a large international marketing services group? Is it a smallish independent? Who runs the company? Does it have a reputation for creativity? Is it strong in television? What are its most famous campaigns? Does it specialize in any niches such as financial services or healthcare? If you can answer these questions and have some knowledge of the issues facing the industry as a whole, you'll be a serious candidate.

Paradoxically, many jobs in advertising are not actually advertised so it is essential to network and make use of any relevant contacts you have. And it is definitely worthwhile sending your CV directly to an agency and enquiring whether they have any vacancies. If you're in the right place at the right time you may well find yourself invited for an interview. This almost certainly won't happen at once, but don't give up. And remember to follow up your letters. It will prove you are eager and persistent – but be careful not to overdo it and stray into pushiness. You're selling yourself, not second-rate double glazing or dodgy timeshares.

Account handling is the one area of advertising where the larger agencies operate a formalized annual recruitment programme. The Institute of Practitioners in Advertising (IPA) keeps a list of agencies looking to recruit account handlers. The vast majority of account handlers are graduates, but IPA research has shown that their choice of degree subject is, by and large irrelevant. For most ad agencies your personality and intelligence are of far greater interest than what you've studied.

The leading agencies may have as many as 2,000 applications for between three and six graduate account-handling jobs. As account handling is essentially about team work most of the agencies that recruit graduates annually ask the best twenty to thirty candidates in for a day, split them into teams, give them objectives to meet and watch how they work together. In this way they can identify the people who are good at solving problems and motivating others and weed out the mavericks, bullies and wallflowers. Be prepared for challenges. Agencies want people able to think laterally and take unusual situations in their stride.

Here's an example that illustrates the attitudes and adaptability agencies regard highly. In 1995 ad agency DMB&B had a graduate intake of four. Instead of asking 'wannabe' employees to fill out a full application form it sent out a shortened version together with a request that applicants make a three-minute video of themselves covering three points: why they should be given a job, their most embarrassing moment and a critique of two press ads included in the application pack. Anyone who didn't make a video or whose video didn't address the three points stipulated was not considered for a job. The agency was also careful not to give any tips on where to borrow a camcorder, making that an extra test of initiative (see chapter 11 for further information on getting a job).

The IPA has recently introduced a clearing-house system for graduates who have made it through to the last phase of the exacting selection processes used by the bigger agencies only to miss landing a job by a whisker. The names of these narrowly unsuccessful applicants are passed to other agencies searching for trainee account-handling staff. The scheme is still in its infancy, and has yet to be embraced by the majority of advertising agencies.

There are no such formalized recruiting procedures for creatives. Copywriters and art directors are hired only when they can demonstrate to an agency's creative director that their work is of a sufficiently high standard. The way most young creatives try to refine their skills is by taking work placements at agencies. This offers them the chance to learn from experienced creatives and to develop their portfolios. The only drawback is that because there are so many young creatives clamouring for the chance to prove their worth, ad agencies can afford to pay them next to nothing. For those good enough to be offered a placement, the harsh reality is that the agency will probably pay them little more than their travelling expenses – perhaps up to £50 a week.

It shouldn't be forgotten that creatives are almost always hired in pairs – an art director teamed with a copywriter – so it is vital to have a creative partner. Some find each other on advertising courses: the most famous, run by West Herts College in Watford, brings art directors and copywriters together to tackle creative briefs and has led to the formation of many partnerships.

If you don't already have a creative partner there are several ways you can go about finding one. You could contact colleges that run courses on advertising, graphic design or creative writing to find out if they have any students thinking about working as creatives. Alternatively, ask your friends if they know anyone who'd fit the bill as one half of the double act you're intending to put together. Or you could even place a small ad in your local newspaper or in a trade publication such as *Campaign*. Finally, the advertising recruitment company Harold MacGregor does some creative matchmaking, putting gifted young copywriters and art directors in touch with one another.

Although most art directors have completed an art or graphics course, copywriters need not have had any special training. What counts above all else is the aptness and originality of the work in your portfolio. Some young creatives try to boost the quality of their work by signing up for a scheme run by the Designers & Art Directors Association (D&AD). It is open to anyone and costs a mere £10 to enter. In return for your money you are set a creative brief by a top ad agency. The agency selects the creators of the best fifteen or so solutions and gives them the chance to attend a series of creative concept workshops held one evening a week and featuring some of the top creatives in the industry. Each week the budding creatives are set a new brief from a different agency and their response to the previous week's brief is criticized. By the end of the six-week course the chances are that they'll have some good ads to show off to potential employers. The D&AD scheme is also a fertile recruiting ground for agencies who are often prepared to give impressive students a chance.

Establishing yourself as a creative is far from easy. It usually means traipsing from agency to agency with your portfolio in the hope that senior creatives will make the time to see you and your ideas. If and when they do, they may be brutal in their criticism. It can be hurtful, but if they are constructive there is no better way to learn. Many would-be creatives have to struggle in this fashion for up to a year or more before landing their first full-time job. Even then starting salaries may be as low as £8,000. But if your creative solutions are consistently good then your pay is likely to rise rapidly. Others never make it and end up doing something else. You should weigh up this risk if you're considering a career as a creative.

Account planners are almost exclusively graduates, yet few begin their working lives in planning. Hardly any ad agencies take on first jobbers as trainee planners so most people move into planning after gaining experience in other areas. The most logical route into planning is from market research, although any job that involves an element of strategic planning, such as account handling or working in marketing for a client, is a legitimate springboard.

Academic qualifications are not nearly as important in creative services. It's more a case of tracking down an agency that has a vacancy for, say, a junior for its production department and convincing whoever's doing the hiring that you're the person for the job. The same holds true for film production companies, though here some evidence of an interest in visual arts would not go amiss. Perhaps a tape of a short movie you've made or a selection of photographs you've taken. At the very least you should have some strong critical views on commercials, movies and TV programmes, which should show rather more insight into the filmmaking process than inane burbling on the latest plot twists in *EastEnders*.

Finally, secretarial and administrative jobs: these, too, can be difficult to come by but once you've gained experience of an advertising environment you may find your skills in demand from agencies keen to hire those who know something about their business. And if you do go on to acquire a lot of knowledge about the business there's always the possibility that you could move into other jobs in advertising. This isn't commonplace – with the exception of TV departments/film production. You must remember that agencies can have their pick of top-flight graduates when filling trainee account-handling positions. Even so, if you're willing to learn, have an aptitude for the work and an understanding boss, you might be given a shot. If, however, it looks as if your boss is the type who'll ignore your potential, then gather what useful experience you can before moving to an agency where the outlook is more promising. And take heart: some people now at the top of the industry began their careers as post-room juniors and secretaries.

As for vocational qualifications, art directors and studio designers aside, in the main they are viewed as being of little significance. Having a qualification like CAM may demonstrate a degree of commitment to a career in marketing services but carries little weight with most agency recruiters – certainly far less than for jobs in PR.

Chapter 6 / **Advertising from the Client's Side**

Have you ever heard of a brand of cigarettes called Strand? No? The reason you haven't is its infamously ill-judged 1959 advertising campaign, which featured a lone smoker with the slogan 'You're Never Alone with a Strand'. Consumers concluded that this must mean only saddoes with no friends smoked Strand. The brand's image was destroyed and it disappeared. It's a salutary lesson on the power of advertising, for better or for worse.

Companies create awareness among their target markets by advertising, but they have to think long and hard about what image they want to convey when they do so – the shock tactics of Benetton, the raunchy stylishness of Levi's or the anarchy of Tango would be inappropriate for Marks & Spencer, Persil and Barclays Bank.

Clients can't afford to leave every aspect of an advertising campaign to their agencies. The stakes are too high for that. It would be reckless of them to gamble with their reputations by ceding complete control of a campaign to others, no matter how trustworthy, informed and accomplished they might be. Clients select the agencies they want to work with, brief them and approve or reject the creative and media solutions they devise. But who has this responsibility at the client company? This is where things become complicated. While most advertising agencies have a similar structure, or at least one that bears more than a passing resemblance to that of their rivals, clients are structured in many ways. After all, you wouldn't expect IBM to have the same set-up as Tesco, or Prudential to be like British Gas. They are all big advertisers but they all offer very different products and services.

However, most of the advertising-related jobs at client companies will be within the marketing department, although, occasionally, they may come under sales or a management unit called something like corporate communications – which, as its name implies, will deal with activities such as corporate PR as well. Under the umbrella of marketing, a number of different jobs entail some responsibility for advertising. Most large advertisers have a marketing director and perhaps marketing managers, but whether or not they also have advertising managers or brand managers depends on their corporate culture and the type of business they are in.

But however responsibility for advertising is divided up within an organization, one thing is nearly always true: it is a vitally important part of an organization's marketing and usually has a sizeable budget. According to figures from research company Register-MEAL, in 1994 all of the top 100 advertisers in the UK spent at least £10 million on advertising. Unilever alone spent more than £200 million. The next two, Procter & Gamble and BT, both spent over £100 million.

Brand Managers

One of the most highly competitive areas of business is the fast-moving consumer goods (FMCG) sector: branded packaged products such as foods, drinks and toiletries that sell in huge volumes. For the owners of these brands – often multinational companies such as Nestlé, Unilever, Procter & Gamble, Mars, Heinz, Cadbury Schweppes, Kellogg – marketing is of fundamental importance. It's not an overstatement to say that it drives their business. They need to achieve high levels of brand awareness among consumers in order not to lose market share to rival brands or supermarket own-label products.

Brand managers are responsible for a brand's profits, sales and market share, so the job is far broader than working on advertising and promotions alone. Nevertheless, advertising plays an important role and it is up to the brand manager to ensure that the brand is advertised effectively. This entails working closely with the advertising agency to create campaigns that position the brand in its appropriate target market and help lift or sustain its sales.

The high level of expenditure on FMCG marketing means that the brands are better known than the companies that own them. You'll probably be familiar with most if not all of the following brands, Head & Shoulders, Oil of Ulay, Vidal Sassoon Wash & Go, Ariel, Fairy Liquid, Always, Pampers, Pantene, Camay and Lenor, but may know little about the company behind them, Procter & Gamble.

For the brand manager, a prime consideration is to work out which elements of the marketing mix to use and when, and the weight they are given. That could mean initiating a direct marketing drive or stepping up advertising activity. A brand manager's other duties may include dealing with the sales department to ensure that the brand gains wide distribution and is well presented in stores, and working with the product-development team to create new products for the brand name. She will also have a say on packaging and design and commission consumer research to gauge public perception of a brand.

Brand managers are sometimes called product managers. This title is more common at companies outside the FMCG sector, such as manufacturers of consumer durables like cars, fridges, small appliances and hi-fi equipment and business goods like personal computers. It also describes those within financial services companies engaged in marketing, for example, different insurance products.

As a brand/product manager you need to be able to think strategically, to be innovative, analytical and a good communicator. You should be an adept co-ordinator and team leader: you may be in charge of some assistants and carry responsibility for their performance, training and career development. You will probably report either to a group product manager or marketing manager. These more senior positions involve more strategic thinking and responsibility for the performance of a number of brand teams. A group product manager is likely to have continual contact with her advertising agency. She may, for example, brief account handlers, meet with planners, attend shoots, sign off important ads and monitor the effectiveness of a campaign.

FMCG companies will recruit graduate trainees as assistant brand/product managers at a salary of about £15,000. One or two of the leading brand owners may pay top graduates £17–18,000. A senior brand/product manager may earn £30,000 and a group product manager £28–45,000.

Johanna Patterson

Age : **29**
Job title : **Senior product manager, moulded range**
Employer : **Cadbury**
Salary : **Mid £30,000s**
Academic qualifications : **BA (Hons.) business studies**

'I joined Eden Vale in September 1988 as a management trainee working as assistant brand manager on the Ski brand. While at Eden Vale I also worked in National Accounts, on both branded and own label business, with J. Sainsbury and Tesco. I also had extensive exposure to all other grocery accounts in a new product-development role.

'In July 1991 I joined Scott Ltd as product manager on the leading international baby wipes brand Baby Fresh and had extensive dealings with both Europe and the US. In June 1993 I moved on to Andrex toilet tissue – a brand worth over £200 million – as senior brand manager. I worked on the Andrex *Puppy Book* promotion which received four Institute of Sales Promotion Awards in 1994.

'In June 1994 I moved to Cadbury as senior brand manager on the Caramel and Fry's brands and the grocery range. Just over a year later I was given a new role with responsibility for Cadbury's flagship brand, Dairy Milk, and the moulded range, including Fruit & Nut and Whole Nut.

'I am responsible for delivering the volume and profit objectives for the moulded range and managing a marketing budget of several million pounds in order to achieve this. I'm also responsible for market research, advertising and initiating new product developments. My job involves a high level of number manipulation, from budget control to promotional costings and forecasting volumes.

'I start work at about eight-thirty and finish around seven. FMCG is a highly competitive area and you have to work hard – but it's very varied and enjoyable. One of my greatest achievements was the TV-supported "Race the Ace" promotion. Consumers had to collect twenty Cadbury's wrappers to get a free trial on a go-kart track. The fastest man and woman at each circuit got a chance to race against Nigel Mansell at Brand's Hatch. The finals were excellent and "Race the Ace" proved to be one of the most successful promotions Cadbury has ever run.'

Advertising Manager

Some client companies, particularly retailers, employ advertising managers. This job title sounds similar to that of advertisement manager, which refers to someone in charge of a team selling advertising space, so it is important not to get the two jobs confused. An advertising manager at a client company does a very different job from an ad manager in media sales: the essence of her job is to co-ordinate much of her company's day-to-day advertising activities.

Because of the nature of their business, large retailers have a special need for such co-ordination. Even national retailers do lots of local advertising, either to support new store openings or to attract consumers to established stores. These ads almost invariably include local store details, such as its address and directions for reaching it, and often contain some pricing information or details of special offers, which might be subject to change at the last minute. All of this amounts to a lot of work for the retail multiples, like the supermarket and DIY chains – hence the existence of advertising managers.

As an advertising manager you liaise with advertising agencies and media specialists. You will brief the creative agency, and make sure they come up with an acceptable solution and meet their deadline. You will also check the copy for errors, at the same time ensuring that the media agency has secured space in the most appropriate media and at a good price. Due to its often short lead times, the job can be frenetic. To do it well you will need to be decisive, meticulous and calm under pressure.

Large advertisers who have several agencies working on different brands, products or services may also have an advertising manager whose job is to manage the relationships with these 'roster' agencies – BT, for instance, employs someone in such a capacity. These advertising managers take an overview of all of the client's advertising, liaise with both marketing personnel and agency staff to establish that everyone is happy with the way things are going. They may also be involved in the selection of agencies and the drafting of their contracts. Salaries are around £30,000.

Media Manager

Some large advertisers, such as National Lottery operator Camelot, employ a media manager, whose role is to concern herself specifically with media planning and buying. She keeps in continual contact with agency media planners and buyers – the planning and buying may be done by separate agencies – paying keen attention to what is going on with budgets and scheduling.

She may talk to her media agency as many as half a dozen times a day. There will also be regular meetings between her and the planners and buyers where she will outline in general or specific terms when and where she wants the advertising to appear. Her job may also entail sounding out brand managers or marketing managers for their input.

Most media managers come into the job after working first for an advertising agency or media specialist. They may earn £25–45,000.

Marketing Manager

You will find marketing managers at all sorts of organizations, from airlines to banks, telecommunications companies to hotel groups, component manufacturers to record labels. Their seniority and place in the hierarchy depends on the structure of the company, but it is often an important job in which the incumbent may report straight to the marketing or commercial director.

At an FMCG company a marketing manager is senior to a brand manager. She may be responsible for several brand-management teams, consisting of brand managers and assistant brand managers, will oversee their performance, help their career development, give strategic advice and will take part in important meetings with the advertising agency. She will probably help formulate marketing strategy based on market research.

At non-FMCG companies a marketing manager may have responsibility for marketing specific products or services – or indeed the company as a whole. She may have input on PR, sales promotion and direct marketing as well as advertising. Her job may involve lots of day-to-day contact with these various kinds of marketing agencies. In a business-to-business marketing environment she may have designated major clients or target sectors to which she will promote the company's products or services. In addition, she may have a say in co-ordinating the sales team.

To be an effective marketing manager you need motivational and communications skills and an aptitude for strategic planning. It can be taxing and pressurized but also fast-moving and rewarding. You will be mapping the commercial direction of a product or service and holding down a key central-management role. Salaries are in the range £20–50,000.

Shelley Newton

Age : **35**
Job title : **Marketing communications manager, Dell Direct**
Employer : **Dell Computer Corporation**
Salary : **Over £25,000**
Academic qualifications : **Postgraduate Certificate in Education and a B.Sc. (Hons.) in biological sciences**

'I was a science teacher for a couple of years, which is an excellent foundation for my job now because teachers have to be meticulous and organized. I moved to an IT training company in a role which turned out to be as much about marketing as training. Then I moved to Dell when it was a young, new company ideally placed to provide me with an excellent grounding in a variety of roles.

'My current role involves a busy, deadline-dependent workload that includes managing a variety of agencies and the Dell Direct marketing team. Co-ordination is the key. We all need to work together to ensure the advertising creative is consistent with the needs of the business, depicts the right image and provides up-to-the-minute information, especially on pricing. In addition, once the creative has been agreed I work in conjunction with our media-buying agency to evaluate the publications, timings and budgets for the advertising schedule. It really is a team effort and meeting deadlines is crucial.

'Dell is the worldwide leader in selling direct to its customers and as such the output of my job has a tremendous impact on the business. There really is no room for mistakes and the pace is very fast, as one would expect in an industry growing as quickly as the PC industry.

'The way in which we promote Dell's product offering has evolved in line with the business, and we have joined forces with some of our industry partners to participate in campaigns. Apart from the print media, we advertise on London taxis and have run a large outdoor poster campaign, backed up by comprehensive direct mailing. Direct marketing accounts for the other part of my responsibilities. This is as time-consuming as the advertising and equally demanding, as I manage the team involved in the design, proof-reading, print and distribution of the Dell Direct literature and mail.

'Many people have a view of advertising and marketing as glamorous. In fact it is incredibly hard work but very rewarding.'

Marketing Director

The marketing director has overall responsibility for marketing strategy. Generally she will sit on the board of a company as one of its most influential directors, although she may be junior to a sales or commercial director.

She will have ultimate control of the marketing budget, deciding which elements of the marketing mix to use and when, and how much weight to give each one. More than that, she will oversee product development, positioning in the marketplace and pricing. She may also call the shots on sales policy.

The marketing director, perhaps with the approval of other senior directors like the chairman and/or chief executive, will have the final say on the choice of an advertising agency. She will draw up the brief, setting out the objectives to be achieved through advertising. Then she will pick a shortlist of agencies to pitch for the business, making sure that each is equipped to handle the account and won't already be working for other clients that will present an insuperable conflict of interest. With a handful of her colleagues, she will see the pitches and decide which agency to appoint. She will weigh up several factors before making her selection: an agency's understanding of her company's business and objectives, the quality of its creative solutions, value for money, the experience and ability of the proposed account handlers, the agency's track-record, the research it has undertaken and effort it has put into its presentation. The same holds true for the appointment of media specialists, direct-marketing agencies, sales-promotion companies and often PR consultancies.

She will have the final say in approving creative solutions and important advertising executions such as national press ads or TV commercials. In essence she will be the driving force behind a campaign and may have strong creative ideas of her own as well as on the work of the agency. Due to her senior position she may have meetings and working lunches with agency heads as well as with the account director and her team, and she will be courted by other agencies eager to pick up business from her.

Salaries for marketing directors vary greatly according to their experience and the size of their employer. They may earn £30–45,000 at medium-size companies but substantially more at the UK's biggest corporations – over £100,000 in some cases.

Sue Whitehead

Age : **35**
Job title : **Director of marketing services**
Employer : **Thistle & Mount Charlotte Hotels**
Salary : **Around £30,000**
Academic qualifications : **LCC Business Studies Diploma**

'I worked as a secretary at the Foreign Office for a couple of years but decided I wanted to stay in London, so I joined the White House Hotel as assistant to the deputy general manager. After two years I moved to Holiday Inn as a marketing assistant, which was my first exposure to marketing.

'I spent ten great years at Venice Simplon-Orient-Express in a number of roles, ending up as market-development manager. In 1993 I was posted to Singapore for six months to organize the launch of the Eastern and Oriental Express.

'In my current job I report direct to the chief executive. I'm responsible for all worldwide advertising as well as direct marketing, branding, sales promotion, market research, brochures and other print, exhibitions and relationship marketing – our marketing relationships with our existing customers and other companies. I have to decide which elements of the marketing mix are right to achieve our business objectives. We have over ninety hotels in Britain. Our major markets are the UK, US, Japan, Australasia, Europe and South East Asia and all worldwide marketing is co-ordinated through my department.

'Our advertising has to talk to a number of different audiences – the travel trade, business travellers, leisure clients, companies organizing conferences, meetings, exhibitions and so on. We launched a new corporate identity last year and this has featured in all our recent advertising. We mainly use print media – newspapers and magazines.

'The fit between advertising agency and client is very important, at both a business and personal level. We use the Leith Agency in Edinburgh. I talk regularly to the account team about specific work the agency is doing. I like them to take a broad view, look at the marketplace and make suggestions, as well as taking briefs from me. It should be a two-way street. Our media agency is The Media Shop in Glasgow, but we buy some space ourselves as part of the quite complicated relationships we have with other companies in the travel sector.

'Not having gone to university, I'm pleased to have worked my way up to where I am today. Marketing is an exciting and challenging area, particularly in the travel industry where the product itself is so interesting.'

Laura Cannon

Age : **31**
Job title : **Marketing director, Gossard & Berlei**
Employer : **Gossard International**
Salary : **Over £40,000**
Academic qualifications : **BA (Hons.) in marketing and administration**

'After university I took a year off to travel Europe, much of the time in Italy. My first job was at Van den Bergh as an assistant product manager looking after baking products. I loved that job. I was responsible for things like marzipan and icing.

'A year and a half later I moved to Guinness Brewing as an assistant brand manager in new-product development We were testing products like draught bitter and Enigma to put together a package that could then be handed over to a brand team for a launch. It was brilliant because it taught me about creating a brand, but after a year I thought I was fed up with brands and moved to a small design agency.

'I was there seven months and hated it so I went to the recruitment consultancy Ball & Hoolahan and they advised me that I should work on a brand, though one that wasn't too high-profile so I'd have scope to have some input and make an impact. The first interview they got me was at Gossard and I got the job, starting as brand manager on the Gossard brand in May 1990.

'Gossard was seen as pretty and lacy but not trendy. I set about changing that, and now we run a big brand. I was promoted to marketing manager in the middle of 1993 and then marketing director in July 1994 – the first woman ever on the board of Gossard International.

'I look very much at the long-term strategy for the brands internationally. Advertising is key – it's the area where we spend most of our money and I'm very hands-on, going to pre-production meetings and attending the shoot. We co-ordinate the international advertising out of London through our agency AMV. BBDO.

'I love taking a segment of the market that hasn't been cracked and cracking it, which we've done recently with the Berlei Shock Absorber sports bra. I don't think there are many jobs more exciting than marketing. You've got to love watching people and what they like, and have a lot of drive to be successful in marketing. Don't give up – it took me months and hundreds of applications to get my first job. Make sure you have a good CV, not one that hides your light under a bushel. And if you're lucky enough to get a placement, take it and take it seriously.'

Getting in and Getting Ahead

There is no single route into a career in marketing on the client side. Some people move into it after starting their careers in other parts of a company such as sales, operations or administration. Others work their way up from junior jobs in the marketing department or switch to the client side after beginning in advertising agencies. Another option is to come in on a graduate-trainee programme, for instance as an assistant brand manager.

For those pursuing the latter route, it is possible to rise to brand manager within two to four years – but trainee brand-management jobs go exclusively to graduates. It should also be borne in mind that a life sciences degree may stand you in good stead for a trainee brand job at a pharmaceutical company: the giant drugs companies like SmithKline Beecham and Glaxo-Wellcome own brands every bit as significant as some of the best-known food and drink brands. Owners of other sorts of brands will consider graduates in most subjects, although degrees in business studies and marketing will be viewed favourably.

If you plan to do, or are doing, a degree in one of these subjects, choose your time out on a work placement with care. Pick a company active in a market in which you want to work: if you're set on working in business-to-business IT marketing, get some experience of this kind if you can. Ditto travel, FMCG . . .

There is no more respected on-the-job training in marketing

than that given to graduates starting in brand management. The stiff competition for market-share among brand owners means they rely on expert marketers to look after their brands, and those coming in as trainees are steeped rigorously in marketing methodology and techniques. Many people shown the ropes in brand management go on to apply what they've learnt to building a career in other areas of marketing, but lots more stay in brand management and work their way up to brand manager, marketing manager and – if they are really good – beyond.

Companies in sectors other than FMCG sometimes have vacancies for marketing assistants, who often get a first-rate introduction to the business, learning from senior marketers and getting to sit in on important meetings such as ad agency or PR consultancy briefings. Jobs like this nearly always specify graduates and frequently pay £9–13,000.

That is the direct graduate route into a marketing career. But, as we've already said, it is by no means the only one. The nature of jobs like advertising manager or media manager means they call for a good understanding of how advertising and media agencies work. It will come as little surprise that clients often recruit staff from advertising or media agencies to fill these roles.

If you want to break into marketing from elsewhere within a company, sales offers the best opportunities although many people manage to move into marketing from an operational capacity. Some of those working in the marketing department of a bank, perhaps, will have come in as graduate trainees, others will have moved there from marketing jobs at other companies, still others may have begun by working in a branch, only to gain expertise in a certain product or area that makes them a valuable addition to the marketing team. This sort of career path is the best way into a marketing job for non-graduates. Employers sometimes value relevant business experience more highly than academic excellence.

When job-hunting, you should scan the marketing press for vacancies and news on what the top clients are up to. *Marketing* and *Marketing Week* are the best sources of information. It is worth watching out for *Marketing Week*'s annual survey of the top advertisers and *Marketing*'s annual report on the UK's leading brands to get a feel for those companies most committed to marketing.

The qualifications offered by the Chartered Institute of Marketing (see Qualifications and Courses, Chapter 9) are widely recognized and well regarded. Aside from the credibility it bestows, becoming a member of the CIM has networking advantages: the Institute has forty-three branches that run local and regional initiatives, and has specialist groups for marketers in different industries. As well as the chance to discuss important marketing issues, CIM allows you to build contacts with people who may one day be in a position to give you a job.

Developing good relationships with marketing colleagues is just as important. When a marketing director or other senior marketer moves company it is quite common for her to take one or two valued members of her team with her.

Nissan Micra – Ask Before You Borrow It

Case Study of a Campaign

In January 1993 Nissan Motors (GB) launched its redesigned small car, the Micra. The original Micra had been selling relatively well but its customer profile was quite old. Nissan's marketing department, with its advertising agency TBWA, concluded that an advertising campaign to support the introduction of the revamped Micra should have two main objectives: first, it should announce the new shape to the public; second, with a view to generating long-term sales, it should aim to lower the model's customer-age profile by targeting the restyled car at a younger audience and particularly at young women.

The initial solution was the 'Bubble Shape' campaign. This was extremely successful at drawing consumer attention to the new-look car but both Nissan and its agency felt that more needed to be done to make it an attractive proposition for younger consumers. In March 1994 Stuart Harris Research was commissioned to find out what consumers thought of the Micra and its advertising. Qualitative research was carried out among six groups of eight people (two groups each in London, Glasgow and Edinburgh), drawn from Nissan's target audience for the Micra. The research groups were shown a selection of commercials and pictures.

The findings were that while the 'Shape' campaign had been effective at signalling that Nissan had brought out a new and distinctively styled model, the Micra was still suffering from a 'desirability deficit' among the young women buyers the company wished to attract. What was wanted in the advertising was a storyline with a more emotional message. Clearly it was time for a change in the advertising.

TBWA's senior planner wrote a brief that asked the creative teams to develop a new campaign. It had to illustrate that the Micra is a small city car that performs well on open roads, and do so in a way that showed the car to be 'desirable, young, fun and sexy'. Two different campaigns were developed and further research was carried out in June 1994 to gauge consumer opinion.

The preferred campaign was inspired by stories of young men taking their partners' Micras without asking because they so enjoyed driving the car. Out of this was born the campaign strapline 'Ask Before You Borrow It'. The first commercial to feature this theme was written by creative team Chris Hodgkiss and Pip Bishop, and appeared on UK television screens for the first time on 1 January 1995. 'Tantrum', as the commercial was known, was something of a mini-homage to the French movie *Betty Blue* and portrayed a young woman so angry with her partner for borrowing her Micra without asking that she threw his possessions out of the window of their beach-front home.

'Although the Shape work was extremely successful at telling people the car had changed it didn't really move the target market,' says Pip Bishop. 'The new brief was that the car was aimed at wilder women. We spent a lot of time getting the tone right. When men write ads to appeal to women they often do it in a stereotypical way. As a woman I wanted to put a woman's stamp on the advertising. To show females as confident and in control.'

Research showed that the consumers responded well to the campaign. So Nissan asked TBWA to devise a second execution. A new creative brief was written by the agency's planning department and fed into the creative department. Eight scripts were written, and the one that was deemed best was presented to Nissan. 'Stuntman', as the commercial was called, was written by a young creative team who, at the time, were on a two-week work placement at the agency. The commercial, which you will almost certainly recall, was shot in Hollywood and features a stuntman who takes his girlfriend's Micra to work with him without asking for permission only to be thrown out of the window and into the swimming pool when he returns home. 'Stuntman' first appeared in June 1995 and has been shown on TV and in the cinema.

At the same time as the TV commercials, the campaign message was reinforced with single-page black-and-white ads in women's magazines, including *Cosmo*. The ads, again developed by Hodgkiss and Bishop, were unusual for car ads in that they did not show a car – unless you include the small stylized line drawing of the bubble shape design at the top of the page. Among the executions they devised below the 'Ask Before You Borrow It' strapline were a young hunk recoiling from a blow to the groin, a signed photo of George Best ripped into quarters, an expensive man's watch sizzling in a frying pan and a sleeping lover unaware that half his scalp had just been shaved.

Further research commissioned by Nissan showed consumer recall of the 'Ask Before You Borrow It' strapline to be 34 per cent, which in terms of advertising recollection is very high. Research also found that men agreed that they would like to 'steal' the car and women approved of being shown as independent and assertive. But, most importantly from Nissan's point of view, the Micra has been selling well.

'The "Ask Before You Borrow It" campaign was designed to inject more personality into the Micra, which in its previous model guise had about as much personality as a sack of cement and the looks to go with it,' says Nissan marketing operations manager David Horncastle. 'The "Shape" launch campaign for Micra succeeded in putting the car on the map and getting it noticed, "Ask Before You Borrow It" has taken us further down the track and established Micra as a small car with attitude.

'Since its introduction in January 95 with the "Tantrum" TV commercial we have invested about £6 million in "Ask Before You Borrow It" and achieved our highest ad-tracking scores since we started advertising in 1992. Anecdotally as well, the campaign is clearly striking a chord with younger buyers, both male and female, and sales of the Micra continue to forge ahead – up by another 1,000 units in 1995 over 1994.'

Chapter 7 / Media

In 1995 32,800 sixth formers applied to do media studies at university, another 12,000 for communications courses – you can draw your own conclusions from these figures as to the popularity of careers in media. A high number of these students could end up working on the editorial side as journalists, TV producers and the like, but many others – and plenty more besides who haven't done a media course – will opt for careers on the commercial side.

It's an exciting time to begin a career in media. While the print sector still has the biggest slice of the revenue cake, there has been a tremendous explosion and fragmentation in broadcast media during the last few years. New commercial radio stations have been going on air here, there and everywhere, television has been shaken up by the arrival of a host of satellite and cable channels, on top of which, digital technology is being developed which will give broadcasting capacity for a greater number of television and radio channels. Advertisers are beginning to give serious consideration to the possibilities of new media such as the Internet – Guinness for one has experimented with advertising in cyberspace.

According to Advertising Association figures for 1994, the biggest category in terms of expenditure by advertisers was press display advertising at £3.28 billion. The amounts spent in 1994 on the other main categories of advertising are as follows: television £2.87 billion; classified press advertising £2.32 billion; direct mail £1.05 billion. Spend on the remaining types of advertising came to £646 million, of which outdoor/transport totalled £350 million, radio £243 million and cinema £53 million. You will see from these figures that TV and press are the dominant categories, together accounting for over 80 per cent of advertising media spend.

Without advertising we would have a drastically reduced choice of media, and what little commercial media that remained would be far more expensive than it is today. So, as well as generating revenue for media owners, advertising gives the public greater access to media, the sources of information and entertainment we so enjoy. Not to mention the showcase it offers clients for promoting their products and services.

There are two parties in any media advertising deal: the media owner that sells the space and the advertiser, or its agency, that buys it. Selling and buying are opposite sides of the same coin and have much in common. We'll start with sales because that is where most of the jobs are.

Media Sales

If you stop to think about the different sorts of media you come across in a typical week, you'll begin to get some idea of the many kinds of media sales jobs around. There is advertising space to be filled in consumer magazines, trade journals, national and local newspapers and their supplements, on television and radio, the sides of buses and taxis, on posters and more unusual places like the backs of railway tickets. All of it has to be sold by someone.

Selling advertising space can be rewarding. It's a fast-paced business that offers lots of scope for career development and progression. Plain though it is, there is one glaringly obvious fact that is sometimes overlooked by those straining at the leash to break into the media: the job is all about selling. You have to want to sell. If you don't, chances are you'll find it a miserable way to spend your days – and you probably won't be much good at it. If you do like the idea of selling, then media sales may be right up your street.

Most media owners prefer to take on graduates for their trainee sales positions, or those they deem to be of 'graduate calibre'. By this they mean people with the self-assurance and communication skills of a graduate. Such qualities are vital because you will be selling in the main to senior and experienced people who work either for agencies or directly for a client. These people expect to deal with someone able to talk on the same level as they do.

To get a job in media sales you've got to do your research. Read the relevant trade titles like *Media Week* to get a feel for the market, and find out as much as you can about the job on offer. That in itself, though, isn't sufficient. You've got to sell yourself – after all, how would you expect an employer to believe that you'll be good enough to convince advertisers if you can't persuade them? You will almost certainly be interviewed by a manager working in media sales rather than by somebody in personnel so be ready to face some tough questioning – and to ask some intelligent questions of your own.

Don't be afraid to be yourself. To sell media space effectively you have to build relationships and establish a rapport with clients, something that can't be done unless you let your personality shine through. You also need to be logical, unflappable, persistent and able to cope with being rebuffed. Not everyone you talk to will want to buy an ad.

Print

The overwhelming majority of opportunities to begin a career in media sales are in the print sector. Thousands of publications take advertising, ranging from high-profile national newspapers and consumer magazines to the local and trade press. (There are over 5,000 business and professional publications alone.) All of them employ advertising sales teams to sell display and classified advertising.

Print sales is often used as a springboard into careers in other media but many who start their media sales careers in print choose to stay there because they find it enjoyable. It is, nevertheless, a business with a high staff turnover. Many people working in print sales move from job to job quite quickly, which enables them to accumulate experience fast and throws up vacancies for trainees.

There's a fair amount of scope for finding a job if you've an aptitude for selling. But be warned: there are a few dodgy publishing outfits around. These tend to be young, small companies which pay their sales staff commission only or a nominal basic with commission on top. Steer clear of this sort of company, if you can. Look instead for jobs with publishers who pay a reasonable basic, have a number of titles (or one very strong one!), are well established and offer proper training. You can familiarize yourself with the top publishers by reading *Media Week* and doing a little research of your own.

At first, you'll probably have to do all of your selling over the phone. Many companies expect their salespeople to begin their careers selling classified space before moving on to display sales if they have the aptitude and wish to do so. However, this is not always the case. Irrespective of whether you begin on classified or display, you'll be under pressure from the outset to bring in business. Yet, if you perform well, the prospects for advancement are pretty good.

Many progress to become an advertisement manager on a business or small consumer title after only three or four years' experience, and as such you would be helping to run the sales team and have responsibility for looking after some of your publication's most valued advertisers. Your package would probably include a company car and you'd get to meet clients and take them out to lunch. Some publishing companies now have group sales operations as well, allowing them to do deals with media buyers on space across a number of publications.

An ad-sales executive has to build up relationships with clients and media agencies. She should know the strengths and weaknesses of her publication in comparison with the others in the same market. She should also be able to sell its merits against other media like TV or radio.

Experienced ad-sales people sometimes go on to become magazine publishers. The publisher has overall responsibility for the financial performance and successful positioning of her title. She sets budgets and sales targets but also plans and develops conferences, promotions and events linked to her publication to build its position in the market. She will be too busy to spend much of her time selling but will probably be involved in putting together large deals, like sponsored supplements, and making sure that her publication's most valued advertisers are happy. She also works closely with the editor (the publisher is nearly always the editor's boss) to make sure that the publication is serving the readers they want to attract and hold on to. It is unusual to become a publisher before reaching your early thirties.

Publishers generally report direct to the board. Senior publishers – or, in the case of newspapers, advertisement directors – often sit on the board.

Starting salaries in print ad sales vary but many reputable publishers offer trainees a basic of £10–13,500, with the chance to earn commission of £3–5,000 in the first year. A salesperson with three or four years' experience may earn over £20,000, and sales managers over £20,000 with a company car. Most publishers earn £40,000 upwards.

Carolyn McCall

Age : **34**
Job title : **Advertisement director, *Guardian* and *Observer***
Employer : **Guardian Media Group**
Salary : **Over £75,000**
Academic qualifications : **MA in politics and a BA (Hons.) in history and politics**

'I head a department of about 280 people and I'm responsible for generating revenue. My role is threefold. First, I manage internal staff development. Our biggest and most important asset is people, so training and career development are very important. When we are recruiting a field sales person – someone who goes out and meets clients to sell to them – I do the final interviews. That way I get to meet the people coming into the department.

'The second part of my job is developmental – I work closely with editorial and marketing. We have a department called the product development unit that develops ideas, like the *Guardian*'s listings supplement *The Guide*, and the advertising department is always involved at the start of the creative process. Also, if there's a good idea generated by advertising we'll often talk to editorial to see if we can get it off the ground. That could be, say, a music pull-out on a Friday.

'I'm also responsible for the positioning of the papers with advertisers. I meet with advertising agencies and clients to discuss what's happening. I will sometimes do deals but we've got a whole team of people for that. I ensure that the advertising market is informed about what's going on with the newspapers and communicate our marketing strategy. I love talking about the *Guardian* and the *Observer*.

'The only thing I hate about my job is signing invoices. Other than that it's wonderful. I have such an open brief. I sit on the board, which focuses my mind on revenue but also helps give me a broader perspective. I work incredibly long hours because I often start the day with a breakfast meeting, either out with clients or in the boardroom, and there are a lot of evening functions to go to as well. I'll usually work from about 8.15 a.m. to anywhere between 7 p.m. and 12 p.m. But I try to keep my weekends clear.

'Having a huge amount of energy is fundamental. I do some international travelling. I go to France, where we have a collaboration with the magazine *Madame Figaro*, and to the States. I also go up to the Manchester office where we have fifty-four people in the ad department.

'I was very involved in merging the ad departments of the *Guardian* and the *Observer*. That was a tricky and sensitive time because the *Guardian* had taken over the *Observer*. I spent a lot of time working out how to integrate the two. Now if you go out to the sales team you can't tell who came from which paper. To me that was as much of an achievement as being promoted to advertisement director.'

TV

From the outset it's important to draw a distinction between selling advertising airtime for most cable or satellite channels and selling space for the 'terrestrial' broadcasters, especially ITV. With cable and satellite channels, a harder sell is required because their penetration of the marketplace is nowhere near that of ITV, which, of course, can be seen free of charge by anyone with access to a TV set and whose prime-time offerings deliver millions of viewers at a time to its advertisers.

Selling slots like these is more about negotiation than the hard sell. Advertisers want the space in the commercial breaks of programmes watched by their target audience – but also want to pay as little as they can for it. The sales executive's job is to squeeze out of them the largest possible amount of revenue through negotiation.

As recently as 1989 every one of the fifteen companies with an ITV regional franchise – from Granada to Anglia – had its own in-house sales team. Now, that has been consolidated into three large sales operations, plus Television Sales Scotland, which sell airtime for the ITV companies. One of these is the in-house team at Carlton, which sells airtime for the two franchises it owns, Carlton in London and Central in the Midlands. The other two operations, Television Sales and Marketing Services (TSMS) and Laser Sales, are 'sales houses'. They sell the advertising airtime for all the other ITV regions.

Getting a job with one of the ITV sales operations is no easy matter. There are opportunities, but they are seldom advertised. They go instead to those who have the initiative to track them down. Some people begin their careers working as an assistant whose job is to check schedules, book spots once deals have been done and make sure a campaign has been delivered. The job is computer-intensive but also involves talking to clients on the phone, and as such is a good grounding for sales.

Channel 4, Channel 5 and GMTV, the other terrestrial TV broadcasters, sell their own airtime. Then there are the cable and satellite broadcasters such as Sky, MTV, Eurosport and many others, who all have their own sales operations. Selling airtime for these companies often requires a more aggressive approach, similar to print and radio sales. It is, however, part of a growing market. During 1995 the cable companies spent an estimated £2 billion on connecting homes and while there are only about 2 million subscribers at present, it is estimated that there will be between 4.4 and 7.1 million subscribers by the year 2000. Channels unique to cable include Wire TV, Live TV and The Learning Channel.

One area of TV sales that has really taken off in recent years is broadcast sponsorship, with commercial sponsors paying to lend their names to certain programmes. The skill here is to match sponsors with suitable programmes. Good examples include private healthcare company PPP's sponsorship of medical drama *Peak Practice* and insurance group Commercial Union's £1 million sponsorship of *London's Burning*.

No one's really sure what the arrival of digital television will mean in the longer term but it should lead to the creation of new channels and, hence, further opportunities in TV sales. Time will tell. What is certain is that TV has come a long way since 8.12 p.m. on Thursday 22 September 1955, which was when the first commercial to appear on UK independent television was broadcast. The advertiser and agency were Gibbs SR toothpaste and Young & Rubicam.

Salaries in TV sales begin at about £11,000. Good sales executives could be earning about £18,000 plus large bonuses, after eighteen months or so and account directors up to £90,000.

Debbie Whitehill

Age : **27**
Job title : **Sales account manager**
Employer : **Television Sales Scotland**
Salary : **£25,000**
Academic qualifications : **BA (Hons.) in business studies**

'When I left school I wanted to do a broad degree so I did business studies and specialized in marketing in the fourth year. My first job was at a fashion agency in Glasgow, selling London designer range clothes to shops in Scotland. Then I got a job as a sales executive on a dance/fashion magazine.

'At the beginning of 1991 I moved to STV as a sales assistant, which was basically administrative, and then after six months became a sales executive. I still work for STV but the sales operation has been restructured and I now sell airtime for the Grampian region as well as STV at an operation called Television Sales Scotland.

'TSS has offices in Glasgow and Edinburgh and I work from both. I deal specifically with the media agencies who buy the time for their clients. It's up to me to get the highest amount and to keep them briefed about the programmes coming up and what deals we can do. There's a fair amount of entertaining. Recently we took a group of contacts to see the Scotland versus Tonga rugby game.

'I get a real sense of satisfaction when I do a good deal. You could do a deal worth £250,000 and because of its size you know it's an achievement. But sometimes when you get an advertiser who only advertises late at night and doesn't spend much money it can be just as satisfying when they agree to do it.

'You need a lot of flexibility and you have to juggle things. And you can certainly influence people to spend more money. I'd say to anybody who wants to get into television sales, just keep writing in and showing an interest. Don't be put off if you don't get anywhere at first. Positions do come up and companies are looking for those people who clearly want to get into media above all else.'

Outdoor and Transport

Outdoor contractors lease or own panels which are used to display advertising posters. There are over a hundred outdoor contractors in the UK, including four particularly large operations: Maiden Outdoor, Mills & Allen, More O'Ferrall Adshel and J. C. Decaux. Working in media sales for an outdoor contractor means trying to persuade media buyers to place ads on your panels.

Putting together poster deals can be quite complicated because the buyer takes into account a number of factors other than price. These include the quality of the sites and the size of poster, which can vary in size from a smallish slot on a bus shelter to a huge roadside display. Sizes are measured in 'sheets' and are generally consistent so that media buyers can buy poster space from more than one contractor at a time without having to produce posters of varying sizes. Common poster sizes are four, six, forty-eight and ninety-six sheets. Most of the media planning and buying of poster space is carried out by outdoor specialists (media-buying operations that specialise in posters). Most of the larger poster contractors are members of the Outdoor Advertising Association (OAA).

Transport advertising is frequently lumped with outdoor because there can be some overlap; for example, with advertising campaigns running simultaneously on roadside sites and on posters at railway stations. But transport is a more diverse category than ordinary posters, and some companies specialize in selling space for specific media. Some companies specialize in selling advertising space on buses, ranging from the large T-shaped site on the side of a double-decker to the smaller spots on the front and rear to interior panels.

Other companies, like Barnett's Taxi Advertising and Taxi Media, sell space in or on black cabs. The space ranges from ads on the 'tip-up' seats to an interior leaflet dispenser to a door panel and a 'complete livery', which is the most striking and expensive option because it means painting the advertising on to the body of the cab. United Airlines is one of the best known taxi advertisers: it paid to alter the liveries of 170 taxis, leaving one half black and painting the other half a Big-Apple-cab yellow to publicize its London to New York service.

Other companies specialize in niche transport markets. Examples of this type of advertising medium are mobile trailers, balloons and signs towed behind aircraft. One way into outdoor and/or transport sales is first to gain experience selling space in another medium such as print. But there are also opportunities if you don't have any media sales experience. Contact the OAA for a list of its members or look in the media directory *BRAD* for transport contacts.

Radio

Commercial radio is hot right now. In 1995, it outgunned the BBC for the first time to pick up over 50 per cent of listeners, and its growth seems certain to continue as new stations come on air and existing ones establish themselves further. The increase in share of listeners has attracted more and more advertisers to the medium. National radio revenue rose by 40.2 per cent in 1993 and by a further 23 per cent in 1994. Not at all bad, considering the British economy was a long way from its best during those years.

The boom in listeners and advertising has meant there are probably greater opportunities for a career in radio sales than ever before. Yet it is still by no means easy to land your first job. Although some commercial stations recruit graduate trainees to their sales force, most prefer to hire sales staff who have clocked up some experience working in another medium. So if you're set on getting into radio, your best bet is probably to get some experience selling space for a publication. That said, some stations have jobs for assistants, which can be a stepping-stone into sales. These are rarely advertised and go to those with the determination and single-mindedness to track them down.

To sell radio airtime you've got to be able to get on well with people and acquire a sophisticated understanding of media. You will often be selling your station not just against another station but against other media such as newspapers, magazines or posters. You'll have to argue your case persuasively and keep in mind what the competition has to offer.

As one radio sales director is fond of saying, 'You've got to be proud to say you work in sales.' If you're in any way embarrassed about it, the job is not for you. Sales executives at national commercial stations will earn over £20,000, sales managers over £30,000. Remuneration at local commercial stations tends to be slightly lower.

Francesca Bonn

Age : **40**
Job title : **Group head**
Employer : **Classic FM**
Salary : **Mid £30,000s plus bonus**
Academic qualifications : **O Levels**

'My first job in media sales was at Border TV. Since then I've worked for Central TV and poster contractors More O'Ferrall and Mills & Allen. I even ran the specialist recruitment agency Media Appointments for a year but I found there was too much administration to do there. I wasn't doing enough of what I was good at – wheeling and dealing.

'I joined Classic FM in November 1992, two months after it started. I've got a great love of music and from what I'd heard of Classic it was the type of product for me. The group heads do two jobs at the same time. I have a list of media-buying agencies that I sell to and have my own individual target to meet. But I'm also responsible for seeing that my group reaches its target.

'I go through what my team are doing. If an ad has been carried by, say, Virgin or Capital and not by us we try to find out why. I analyse the number of pieces of business my group is working on and the "conversation rate" – if they're having trouble completing deals I'll help them with their "closing" skills.

'You have to know the station backwards. We have product-knowledge tests where we're asked questions about Classic's programme schedule, different periods of classical music and audience listening figures. I may talk to the promotions department to see if there's a promotion we can put together or talk to an agency to offer one of its clients a chance to sponsor a programme. And although we have a client-services team, I sometimes go to see a client direct.

'The job's creative. It's about coming up with ideas for bringing in money. For example, getting Wall's Ranieri ice cream to sponsor our summer music festival. It is quite stressful and tough. You have to be slightly larger than life. And you need to be persistent because you do get fobbed off. I went through hell and high water during my first six months at Border because there's a lot to learn. But don't give up, and take every opportunity to network and meet agencies and clients.'

Cinema

In 1984 annual UK cinema admissions stood at 54 million. By 1994 this had more than doubled to 124 million. This boom in attendances has encouraged more advertisers to consider cinema as a medium for their campaigns, but despite the multiplex-powered resurgence in the big screen's fortunes, cinema still remains a comparatively small part of media advertising expenditure. What's more, opportunities to get into a career in cinema sales are limited. Cinema Media (formerly Rank Screen Advertising) and Pearl & Dean Cinemas control the UK market, so if cinema sales is where you want to be, that's who you'll have to approach.

As you'll probably have noticed, cinemas run ads from both national and local advertisers and it takes different skills to sell to each. The proprietor of a small restaurant wishing to advertise on cinema screens in her local area is going to have different needs from a consumer-goods company seeking national exposure. So cinema sales executives specialize, some selling to national advertisers, others to local. What you may not have realized is that cinema tickets would almost certainly be more expensive without the revenue generated by selling advertising space in the slots before the feature film.

Media Planning and Buying

Over the last decade there has been a revolution in the way that media is bought. In the early 1980s nearly all media space was purchased by the full-service advertising agencies who also did the creative work. Today, although some advertising agencies still have media departments that are strong in this regard, a huge amount of the space is bought by companies known as media independents or media dependents. Media independents, as the name suggests, are not owned by advertising agencies. Media dependents, though separate arm's-length companies, are owned by advertising agencies.

The reason for the emergence of these specialists is that media-buying decisions are now more complicated than ever before. Media has fragmented and will continue to fragment further as new television channels, radio stations and publications are born, which leaves more advertising options to consider. It takes a lot of data to draw up an advertising schedule because consumers are harder to pin down than they were ten years ago. Consequently, media-buying decisions are taken seriously. And that is what has opened the door for media specialists.

There are three main types of job at these agencies (and at ad agency in-house media departments): research, media planning and media buying. Researchers accumulate data on different media to help the planners and buyers. The planner usually works on a number of accounts, perhaps four or five at a time. Her job is to develop a media strategy for reaching her client's specified target groups. She picks the media for a campaign and decides how it should be used: for instance, whether the ads should be large or small (or long or short) and the timing and weight of the campaign – although, of course, ultimately she takes her instructions from the client.

A planner identifies the most appropriate media for her client's brand or message. She meets with her clients to get details of their product, budget and market. Then she prepares a plan specifying the media to be used, when the ads are to appear and how often, and a rough idea of costs and any discounts available – as a planner you need knowledge of all the different media available. To plan effectively you make use of up-to-date figures on circulation, readership, broadcast audiences and the like supplied by bodies such as BARB and RAJAR (see Glossary p. 152). But analysing historical figures is only part of the process: you must also be aware of anything that may distort usual reading or viewing habits – if a television series which normally has a high audience is scheduled against a major sporting event like the Olympics it may get substantially fewer viewers than usual in that week.

It's a question of weighing up the costs versus the benefits of different media, picking the most suitable solution, drawing up a plan and presenting it to the client. If the client approves it, the planner briefs the media buyer. The brief to the media buyer gives an outline of the media to be used, the budget available, timing of the campaign and an idea of the number and type of viewers/readers the client wants to reach. Buying is the other side of the coin to media sales. Whereas someone selling media space strives to get as much money as possible for it, media buyers work to acquire it for the lowest price they can.

Clearly, negotiating skills are of paramount importance. You need to be aware of any discounts available and be skilled at getting popular slots at the most favourable rates. You will spend a lot of time on the telephone hammering out deals. You should be numerate, with good communication skills and a sharp business sense, extrovert, meticulous, efficient, enthusiastic, ambitious and not a little streetwise.

At some smaller agencies the media planning and buying jobs are combined. You should also be aware that some clients use separate agencies to do their planning and buying. There are also niche agencies like Concord, Outdoor Connection and Outdoor Focus that concentrate on buying poster space – these three have a centralized buying operation known as Blade.

Starting salaries for trainees/assistants are £10–13,500. A media buyer with eighteen months' experience can earn over £20,000, and after four or five years could be on about £28,000. Heads of TV, press buying etc., may earn over £50,000.

Jane Chaplain

Age : **27**
Job title : **Associate director**
Employer : **CIA Medianetwork**
Salary : **Over £25,000**
Academic qualifications : **BA (Hons.) in history and government**

'I started off in media sales – which is quite a common route into media buying – selling space for the *Birmingham Evening Mail* group. I always wanted to get into advertising but couldn't straight away, and I thought this wouldn't do me any harm. I did that for about nine months but I was applying for jobs at agencies all the time. Then I got a job in London for an agency called Clark & Taylor. Essentially I was planning and buying regional media space. My biggest client was Sainsbury's.

'After four years I decided it was time to move on. I joined CIA Medianetwork in April 1994 as head of regional media and became an associate director in December that year. What I do is to find the most efficient and cost-effective way of communicating to my clients' customers. And I assess what potential customers are doing and work out the best way to reach them. For example, if we have a retail client who's opening a store in Bristol I'd assess all the media in the area to find out which are the most appropriate. Then we buy the space we want, which involves negotiating on cost with the owners. The cheaper we get things the more value we're giving our clients.

'I probably spend 50 per cent of my time talking to clients, either going to meetings with them or on the phone. I also spend a lot of time negotiating with publications and co-ordinating things with creative agencies. It's their job to supply the artwork for the space I'm buying so they need to know the sizes required. I really like dealing with clients. It's good when you know that they're happy because you've helped them sell lots of their product. People have misconceptions that this job is all about going out to lunch. In fact, it's incredibly hard work. It's very service-oriented, so if a client phones up at 8 p.m. and says, "I want something tomorrow," you have to do it.'

Getting in and Getting Ahead

Publishing offers the greatest number of opportunities for launching a career on the advertising side of media. The sheer number of titles and the frequency with which people move around from one to another means there is a fairly steady stream of vacancies for new talent. Many of these vacancies are advertised in national newspapers such as the *Guardian* and in the trade press, but many more are not. It is a case of tracking them down. Pump any contacts you have to find out about jobs – many are put up on a company's noticeboard instead of being advertised externally. Read the media and marketing press to keep up to date with what's happening in the industry: if a publisher is launching a new title it will probably need to recruit more sales staff.

You can find out details of existing publications from sources such as the directory *BRAD*. It lists information on publications like the publishing company's name, address and telephone number, its circulation, advertising rates and often the name of its advertising manager/director or publisher. Ring the publication to check that these names are correct and which of them is responsible for recruiting sales staff, then send them your CV and covering letter. If you haven't heard back from them within a few weeks, which is quite likely, follow up your letter with a phone call. You need to be persistent. If she says she is not hiring, ask whether she knows if any of the company's other publications are taking on junior sales staff or, indeed, if she is aware that any other publisher is recruiting. Most people in sales have friends or acquaintances in similar jobs at rival companies, and many are happy to help if they can. Work on the principle that if you don't ask for help you won't get any.

If you can get some experience selling space for a reputable publishing company – and you're good at it – you'll be well placed to build a good career. You could choose to stay in the print sector, where the opportunities are greatest, or use your experience to move into another medium like poster or radio sales. Alternatively what you have learnt may stand you in good stead for a move into media buying.

There are also junior vacancies in radio and TV sales operations. These are hardly ever advertised, so to get in you have to contact the company's sales director and convince her you have what it takes to make a good salesperson. Be persistent but don't overdo it to the extent of becoming an unwelcome irritant. Unlike in publishing, where trainees begin selling quickly, entry level jobs in radio and television advertising are more often administrative in nature – but they offer an unparalleled means of learning about the business.

Media sales is all about bringing in business and closing deals. That cannot be over-emphasized. The hard fact is that if you don't sell you won't hold down your job for long. Media owners depend on advertising revenue and they can be quite ruthless with those who aren't generating enough of it. You should mull this over when considering whether a career in media sales is the right one for you. On a more positive note, if you do have an aptitude for selling there are tremendous possibilities. Who knows, maybe one day you'll wind up as the publisher of *Cosmopolitan*.

Some of the bigger media specialists take on a handful of trainees every year. Again, these positions are rarely advertised and it's a case of wearing out your shoe leather and writing until your hand aches to land yourself an interview, but if you have enough talent and gumption you should be able to get one in the end. A typical entry level job would be working as a media assistant shadowing a planner or buyer.

Do your homework before any interviews. Read up on what's been going on in the industry in publications like *Media Week*, *Campaign*, *Marketing* and *Marketing Week*. Take note of the latest advertising campaigns and the media on which they have been executed. Whenever you see an eye-catching poster, striking newspaper ad or amusing or original TV commercial, think about what it is advertising. Does the ad work on that medium? If so, why? Could it work better in another medium? What do you think about new media like the Internet? You'll need to have views on these things if you're to convince an employer you're serious about working in media buying. You've also got to be positive, open-minded and have taken the trouble to learn a bit about the industry.

Every year *Campaign* lists the top fifty media agencies as part of its survey on the leading advertising agencies. It may be worthwhile tracking down this issue to find out where in the rankings a particular agency stands. Research company Register-MEAL may also be able to supply you with the latest media expenditure figures for certain advertisers and the billings of media companies on the understanding that this information is not used for commercial purposes. You should also try to find out whether an agency has a reputation for its planning, its buying or both.

Increasingly media sales and buying are becoming graduate careers. There are, however, no hard and fast rules and many employers are open-minded enough to hire people without degrees if they think they have the necessary skills. Once you're in it's your experience that counts. And aside from proving yourself good at your job the way to get ahead is to network. In media, whom you know is almost as important as what you know. So attend all the useful functions you can and work on developing your contacts.

Finally, turn to chapter 11 for more tips on hunting for and landing a job.

Chapter 8 / **Personal Qualities**

It is always dangerous to generalize but some qualities are applicable to the majority of jobs described in this book. A number, of course, will be more appropriate for some jobs than others. Here, though, are the sorts of qualities employers in PR and advertising are looking for:
- Excellent communication skills
- Good written and spoken English
- Persuasiveness
- Interpersonal skills
- Ability to convey ideas
- Ability to empathize with/relate to a target audience
- Good presentation skills
- Leadership and motivational qualities
- Team player
- Respond well to pressure
- Quick thinking
- Assertive and positive – but not domineering
- Flexibility
- Confidence and self-belief
- Capacity to handle criticism and rejection
- Commitment and enthusiasm
- Creative thought
- Understanding of business
- Ability to work to budgets and deadline
- Common sense and logic
- Analytical and problem-solving skills
- Eye for detail
- Numerical and administrative proficiency
- Ability to listen to and absorb what others are saying.

Chapter 9 / **Qualifications and Courses**

Traditionally the businesses of public relations and advertising have relied on the 'working your way up the career ladder' approach rather than insisting on formal academic qualifications. This is partly because of the creative side of both PR and advertising, but also because, unlike regulated professions like the law, formal qualifications have not been a prerequisite of getting a job. The majority of people working in PR or advertising either have degrees in arts or science subjects, which are unrelated to the industry, or no degree at all, having started as a junior and taken it from there.

In public relations in particular, this is changing, not least because the industry is working hard to prove that it should be taken seriously, and that proper standards of education and training are vital in achieving this. Employers increasingly insist on their graduate intake having PR qualifications, and there is now a growing range of courses and degrees from which to choose.

Advertising agencies – with a few exceptions – often look down on advertising-related qualifications. However, if you're planning to work in advertising on the client side, professional qualifications may stand you in good stead. CAM, the Communication Advertising and Marketing Education Foundation, is able to provide details of *National Vocational Qualifications* (NVQs) and their Scottish equivalents, *SVQs*, which are still comparatively new, having only been introduced in November 1994. They run parallel to those traditionally awarded by CAM: the *Certificate in Communication Studies* and the *Diploma* in Advertising or PR. The Certificate forms Part One of the CAM qualification, the Diploma Part Two. When you register with CAM, you will be sent a list of colleges offering tuition. It is also possible to study for the CAM qualifications from home or by attending short, intensive courses. Candidates must have worked in either advertising, PR or marketing for at least a year, should be at least eighteen and have either five O levels or GCSE passes, grades A–C, or two A levels and three O levels or GCSEs, grades A–C, or a BTEC/SCOTVEC Certificate or Diploma in Business Studies, or a degree from a recognized university. Candidates with fewer than five O levels or GCSE passes are allowed to enter only if they have at least three years' relevant work experience.

To get the certificate you must sit and pass six three-hour papers on different subjects: Marketing, Advertising, Public Relations, Media, Sales Promotion and Direct Marketing, and Research and Behavioural Studies. It is recommended that candidates devote at least thirty hours' study time to each subject.

The Diploma examinations are open to candidates who have already obtained the Certificate or an academic qualification that gives exemption from Part One, of which CAM can supply details. All candidates for the Diploma must take the Management and Strategy paper, plus two others. For those working in PR the two relevant papers are Public Relations – Management, and Public Relations – Practice. Those working in advertising take Advertising – Consumer, and Advertising – Business to Business.

The Chartered Institute of Marketing (CIM), which has been in existence for over eighty years and is Europe's largest professional marketing body with over 50,000 members and students, offers a number of well-regarded qualifications. Its entry level qualification is the *Certificate in Marketing*, which covers four main areas: business communications, understanding customers, marketing environment and marketing fundamentals. It is open to those aged eighteen or over with at least four GCSE passes and one A level or one year's relevant work experience. Contact CIM for further details of entry requirements.

The level two CIM qualification is the *Advanced Certificate in Marketing*, which again encompasses four areas: marketing operations, promotional practice, effective management for marketing, and management information for marketing and sales. Entry is open to holders of the CIM certificate or to holders of a degree, HND/C, or NVQ/SVQ level three in an appropriate subject. Those with membership qualifications of other chartered professional bodies or with approved experience in sales or marketing may also be allowed direct entry. Again, contact CIM for details. Advanced Certificate holders can apply for associate membership of CIM.

The level three CIM qualification is the *Diploma in Marketing*. This covers marketing communications strategy, international marketing strategy, strategic marketing management, planning and control, and analysis and decision. Entry is open to holders of the Advanced Certificate, or a business-related first degree with some marketing content, or a number of other qualifications about which CIM can offer advice. The Diploma is an internationally recognized qualification. Successful candidates are entitled to use the designatory letters DipM after their names and may apply for membership of the Institute.

For further information contact:

CAM Foundation (The Communication Advertising and Marketing Foundation)
Abford House, 15 Wilton Road, London SW1V 1NJ
Telephone: 0171 828 7506
Can give information on study through college attendance, home or distance-learning.

Chartered Institute of Marketing
Moor Hall, Cookham, Maidenhead, Berkshire SL6 9QH
Telephone: 01628 524922
Information on evening classes or self-study distance-learning for the General Marketing Diploma.

Public Relations Consultants' Association (PRCA)
Willow House, Willow Place, London SW1P 1JH
Telephone: 0171 233 6026
Runs a careers hotline. Also runs the Public Relations Diploma distance-learning programme for the Public Relations Education Trust (PRET), a joint initiative with the Institute of Public Relations. The diploma enables you to sit for exams leading to the CAM Public Relations Diploma, with no time restraint – good for busy people working full-time who want to improve their skills/qualifications. See also the joint PRCA Diploma in International Public Relations at West Herts College.

PR, Advertising, Graphic Design & Marketing Courses

Cathy Ace & Associates
106 Christchurch Hill, Christchurch Road, London SW2 3UD
Telephone: 0181 671 0584
CAM Certificate and Diploma: distance-learning/intensive study weekends (courses held in Central London).

Bournemouth University
Weymouth House, Talbot Campus, Fern Barrow, Poole, Dorset BH12 5BB
Telephone: 01202 524111
Advertising Management (BA (Hons.)); Creative Advertising Design (BA (Hons.)); International Marketing Management (BA (Hons.)); Public Relations (BA (Hons.)) – four year undergraduate course with third year spent on placement.

Bradford & Ilkley Community College
Great Horton Road, Bradford, West Yorkshire BD7 1AY
Telephone: 01274 753026
Business Administration/Marketing (BA (Hons.)).

Bristol, University of the West of England
Frenchay Campus, Coldharbour Lane. Bristol BS16 1QY
Telephone: 0117 656261
Business Studies/Marketing (HND); Visual Communications & Graphic Design (HND).

University of Central England in Birmingham
Perry Bar, Birmingham B42 2SU
Telephone: 0121 331 5000
Marketing with either Business Administration, Business Information, Economics, European Studies, International Finance, Law or Management (HND).

University of Central Lancashire
Lancashire Business School, Department of Journalism, University of Central Lancashire, Preston PR1 2HE
Telephone: 01772 893730/01772 201201
Combined honours degree in Public Relations. Three-year undergraduate course including placement opportunities.

Cranfield University
Cranfield MK43 0AL
Telephone: 01234 751122
Marketing & Food Management (B.Sc. (Hons.)) – four-year sandwich course.

Croydon College
Fairfield, Croydon CR9 1DX
Telephone: 0181 686 5700
Graphic Design (HND).

De Montfort University
The Gateway, Leicester LE1 9BH
Telephone: 0116 2551551
Graphic Design (BA/BA (Hons.)).

University of Derby
Kedleston Road, Derby DE22 1GB
Telephone: 01332 622222
Graphic Design (BA (Hons.)).

Dublin Institute of Technology
Aungier Street, Dublin 2, Republic of Ireland
Telephone: 010 353 1 4785252
Diploma in Public Relations – one-year postgraduate course with two to four weeks spent on placement after finals.

Dundee Institute of Technology
Bell Street, Dundee DD1 1HG
Telephone: 01382 308000
Marketing, Management & Consumer Electronics (BA/BA (Hons.)).

Falkirk College of Technology
Grangemouth Road, Falkirk, Scotland FK2 9AD
Telephone: 01324 624981
BA in Communication. A new course has been added with a strong emphasis on PR/advertising/marketing. Validated by the Open University.

Falmouth College of Arts
Wood Lane, Falmouth, Cornwall TR11 4RA
Telephone: 01326 211077
Advertising, Copywriting & Art Direction (HND); Graphic Communication (BA (Hons.)).

University of Glamorgan
Treforest, Pontypridd, Mid Glamorgan CF37 1DL
Telephone: 01443 480480
Marketing (BA); Marketing with Languages (BA).

University of Greenwich
Wellington Street, Woolwich, London SE18 6PF
Telephone: 0181 316 8590
Advertising & Design (BA); Business & Marketing Communications (BA); International Marketing (BA); Media & Communication (BA); Advertising Design (HND).

Henshall Centre
Bridge Mount, Jackson's Lane, Hazel Grove, Stockport, Cheshire SK7 5JP
Telephone: 0161 440 8466
A programme of short courses for in-service professional development, covering public relations skills, techniques and management.

University of Huddersfield
Queensgate, Huddersfield HD1 3DH
Telephone: 01484 422288
Marketing (BA/BA (Hons.)); Marketing, Retailing & Distribution (BA/BA (Hons.)); Marketing with a Modern Language (BA/BA (Hons.)).

University of Humberside
Milner Hall, Cottingham Road, Hull HU6 7RT
Telephone: 01482 440550
European Marketing (BA/BA (Hons.)) – specializing in either French, German or Italian.

Industrial Society
Peter Runge House, 3 Carlton House Terrace, London SW1Y 5DG
Telephone: 0171 839 4300
One-day course entitled 'Media Matters' on how to deal with the media.

Institute of Public Relations (IPR)
The Old Trading House,
15 Northburgh Street,
London EC1V 0PR
Telephone: 0171 253 5151
Careers counselling, workshops, seminars and conferences.

Keele University
Staffordshire ST5 5BG
Telephone: 01782 621111
Marketing & Physics (BA); Marketing & Russian (BA); Marketing & Russian Studies (BA) – all four years. Law & Marketing (B.Sc.) – three years.

Lancaster University
The University, Lancaster LA1 4YW
Telephone: 01524 65201
Advertising & Marketing (BA (Hons.)); Marketing with Chinese Studies (BA (Hons.)).

Lansdowne College
7–9 Palace Gate, London W8 5LS
Telephone: 0171 581 4866
Full- and part-time courses in PR, Media, Marketing and Advertising – CAM, CIM and LCCI.

Liverpool John Moores University
4 Rodney Street, Liverpool L3 5UX
Telephone: 0151 231 2121
Marketing & Media & Cultural Studies (Joint Hons.); Marketing & Product Design (Joint Hons.); Marketing & Screen Studies (Joint Hons.); Marketing & Visual Studies (Joint Hons.).

Leeds Metropolitan University
Faculty of Business, 4 Queen Square, Woodhouse Lane, Leeds LS2 8AB
Telephone: 0113 2832600
BA (Hons.) in Public Relations – three- or four-year undergraduate course with third year spent on placement if four-year course followed.

London College of Printing & Distributive Trades
Elephant and Castle, London SE1 6SB
Telephone: 0171 735 8484
Advertising & Marketing (HND); Marketing & Advertising (HND); Marketing, Press & Public Relations (HND).

London School of Public Relations
David Game House, 69 Notting Hill Gate, London W11 3JS
Telephone: 0171 221 3399
'A Comprehensive Introduction to Public Relations' – evening course.

Manchester Metropolitan University
Aytoun Building, Manchester M1 3GH
Telephone: 0161 247 6050/0161 247 2000
MA in Public Relations – one-year postgraduate course with optional 6–8 week placements. Also, Certificate of Higher Education in Marketing Communications.

Middlesex University
All Saints, White Hart Lane, London N17 8HR
Telephone: 0181 362 5000
Marketing (BA/BA (Hons.); B.Sc.

(Hons.)) – available in combination with another subject as part of a joint programme.

Napier University
Print Media, Publishing and Communications Department
10 Colinton Road, Edinburgh
EH10 5DT
Telephone: 0131 444 2266
BA in Communication – three-year undergraduate course with no placement year.

University of Northumbria at Newcastle
Ellison Building, Ellison Place, Newcastle upon Tyne NE1 8ST
Telephone: 0191 227 4064
Marketing (BA/BA (Hons.)).

The Oxford Publicity Partnership
12 Hid's Copse Road, Cumnor Hill, Oxford OX2 9JJ
Telephone: 01865 865466
Variety of short courses in all aspects of publicity, marketing, and copywriting.

University of Paisley
High Street, Paisley, Renfrewshire, Scotland PA1 2BE
Telephone: 0141 848 3000
Marketing (BA/BA (Hons.)).

University of Reading
PO Box 217, Reading RG6 2AH
Telephone: 01734 875123
Typography & Graphic Communication (BA (Hons.)).

College of St Mark and St John
Derriford Road, Plymouth PL6 8BH
Telephone: 01752 777188
BA (Hons.) in Public Relations – three-year undergraduate course with third year spent on placement.

University College Salford
Frederick Road, Salford M6 7PU
Telephone: 0161 736 6541
Graphic Design (BA (Hons.)).

Southampton Institute of Higher Education
East Park Terrace, Southampton, Hampshire SO9 4WW
Telephone: 01703 319000
Corporate Communications (BA (Hons.)/BA (Hons.) Foundation)); Marketing (BA (Hons.)); Marketing Design (BA (Hons.)/BA (Hons. Foundation)); Product Design with Marketing; (BA (Hons.)); Graphic Design (BA (Hons.) Foundation/HND)); Communications (HND).

Staffordshire University
College Road, Stoke on Trent
ST4 2DE
Telephone: 01782 744531
Marketing (BA/BA (Hons.)).

University of Stirling
The University, Stirling, Scotland
FK9 4LA
Telephone: 01786 473171/467380
Film & Media Studies/Marketing (BA); Marketing (BA); Marketing with either Business Law, French, German, Japanese, Psychology, Social Policy, Sociology, Spanish or Sports Studies (BA); Public Relations (M.Sc.) – one-year postgraduate course with non-compulsory placements taking place during March, full-time or distance-learning.

University of Strathclyde
Marketing Department, Sternhouse Building, 173 Cathedral Street, Glasgow G4 0RQ
Telephone: 0141 552 4400
BA in Marketing – three-year course or four years for BA (Hons.).

Swansea Institute of Higher Education
Townhill Campus, Townhill Road, Swansea, West Glamorgan SA2 0UT
Telephone: 01792 203482
Visual Arts, Design & Media Studies (BA (Hons.)) – modular course with options including graphic design or photography.

University of Teesside
Middlesbrough, Cleveland TS1 3BA
Telephone: 01642 218121
Marketing (BA).

Trident Training Services
London House, 68 Upper Richmond Road, London SW15 2RP
Telephone: 0181 874 3610
Intensive tailor-made public relations courses on all different aspects of the business for all different types of clients.

Trinity and All Saints, University of Leeds
School of Media, Brownberry Lane, Horsforth, Leeds LS18 5HD
Telephone: 0113 2837100
BA (Hons.) in Public Media – three-year modular degree scheme including two six-week placements.

University of Ulster
School of Behavioural and Communication Sciences University of Ulster at Jordanstown, Newtownabbey, County Antrim BT37 0QB
Telephone: 01232 328515
Communication, Advertising & Marketing (B.Sc. (Hons.)) – four-year sandwich course including an industrial studies diploma.

University of Wales
School of English Studies, Communications and Philosophy Bute Building, King Edward VII Avenue, Cathays Park, Cardiff CF1 3NB
Telephone: 01222 388621
Postgraduate diploma: Public and Media Relations – one-year course including 200 hours of work placement. The only postgraduate diploma recognized by the IPR.

West Herts College, Watford
Hempstead Road, Watford, Herts WD1 3EZ
Telephone: 01923 257569/257500
Post-Graduate Diploma in Copywriting/Art Direction – full-time 36-week course (BTEC) which has been running since 1961 and is the most famous in the industry. Advertising (HND); Advertising Management (HND): Marketing Management (HND). Watford/Public Relations Consultants Association (PRCA) Diploma in International Public Relations – one-year postgraduate course with two to three weeks during May spent on placement, usually in France.

PR Consultancy Training Programmes

Biss Lancaster Plc
69 Monmouth Street, London
WC2H 9DG
Telephone: 0171 497 3001
In-house (graduate) training programme.

Burson-Marsteller Ltd
24–28 Bloomsbury Way, London
WC1A 2PX
Telephone: 0171 831 6262
Burson-Marstellar, the world's largest public relations company, has an annual recruitment programme supplemented by a minimum of 30 hours' annual in-house training for all personnel.

Daniel J Edelman
Kingsgate House, 536 King's Road, London SW10 0TE
Telephone: 0171 835 1222
In-house (graduate) training programme.

Harvard Public Relations
Harvard House, Summerhouse Lane, Harmondsworth, West Drayton, Middlesex UB7 0AW
Telephone: 0181 759 0005
In-house (graduate) training programme.

Shandwick Public Relations
87 Vincent Square, London
SW1P 4ES
Telephone: 0171 835 1001
In-house (graduate) training programme.

TV Production

No formal qualifications are needed but if you can get yourself on a reputable and relevant course you'll have the edge over those without any experience.

Skillset
The industry training organization for broadcast, film and video (see Useful Addresses, p. 178) was set up in 1992 by the film and TV industry, including independent production companies, to develop relevant qualifications. You should contact Skillset for the latest information on courses and qualifications. One of the most highly rated courses is run by FT2.

FT2
4th Floor, 5 Dean Street, London
WIV 5RN
Telephone: 0171 734 5141
Film and Television Freelance Training (FT2) has approximately 25 places on its course, a two-year introduction to working in technical and production jobs in television. Enthusiasm for TV/film counts for as much as academic qualifications in getting on the course, which is always oversubscribed. Contact the administrator for details.

Chapter 10 / **Guide to the Jargon**

PR

account   Every PR consultancy has clients, and each client project becomes an account worked on by an account executive, manager and/or director.

advertorial   A newspaper or magazine advertisement designed to look like a feature.

angle   What journalists look for and PRs must provide, also known as 'hooks' or 'pegs'. An angle gives journalists reason to cover a story and mention your product/person/idea/organization/theme. This could be something as simple as your event being timed to coincide with a major anniversary.

airtime   Literally, the amount of time on the airwaves, either TV or radio.

artwork   Visual material ready to use in print or on TV.

biog   Written biographical information, handed out as necessary or included in a press kit.

briefing   Either a written or verbal presentation providing background information, either for the media, or your own boss or client.

Campaign   The beginning, middle and end of a particular project for your client or company. A campaign can last for days, weeks or even years, but it always has a specific objective, whether it's launching a brand of soap or trying to legalize something in Parliament.

client list   PR consultancies often send out lists of all their clients when they are pitching for new business or publicizing their own.

clip   TV or radio segment for broadcast as part of overall programme.

columnist   National and local newspapers have journalists who write regular columns, and sometimes commission celebrities or politicians.

correspondent A journalist who reports on a specific subject, from beauty to boxing.

consultancy Generally speaking, there are ad agencies and PR consultancies. Companies often approach PR consultancies for strategic advice – pure consultancy – rather than project work, which they can often do internally. PR consultancies also offer a full range of PR services.

contacts People you get to know personally in your business and the media are contacts, and they are the lifeblood of any good PRO.

corporate identity What a company says about itself and how it says it are part of the perception the public or its customers have of its corporate identity. 'The Bank that Likes to say Yes' is both a slogan and a corporate identity; so are the colours used on headed writingpaper or invitations.

corporate hospitality Entertainment in private boxes at big public events like Wimbledon or the Proms, held by companies or organizations to entertain their clients, associates or the media.

cover-mount Increasingly, glossy magazines are being published with books, tapes or other products like shampoo stuck or 'cover-mounted' on the front, as a free gift for the reader.

crisis management Tactics to handle the media and other 'publics' when the unexpected or the worst happens. Works to present the company or client in the clearest way to avoid more damage by speculation and adverse coverage.

database Computer system for contacts. Most companies and consultancies have their own database, but there is a range of media databases to which you can subscribe if you want more names and contacts.

deadline The date on which journalists must have submitted their copy.

diary Another word for newspaper gossip column.

dipCAM A qualification awarded by the CAM Foundation (Communication, Advertising and Marketing Education Foundation), which is widely respected.

down-the-line When a spokesperson can't get an interview themselves, the interview can be done 'down-the-line' either by telephone, or satellite or fibre optics.

electronic media TV radio or computer media such as the Internet.

embargo Request to editors and producers not to use the information you give them before a certain date and time, when you need to alert them to it in advance so that they can prepare their coverage. Most good journalists respect embargoes, but not all.

endorsement quote Getting a product or idea endorsed by celebrities or opinion-formers is often a good way of attracting PR coverage.

exclusive 'Scoop' is now unfashionable and instead the media uses 'exclusive', meaning that a story is being given to one medium before anyone else.

expenses Records of what is spent on behalf of a project or client.

feature Coverage that is not news, and has different potential for promoting a product or subject.

fees PR consultancies charge fees for each client project. These range in size depending on the project, how long it lasts and how many staff will be needed.

freelance Journalist or PR who is not employed by any one company or organization.

footage TV or radio material for broadcast.

follow-up Chasing up contacts after initial approach (could be media, for example).

forward planning Newsrooms in newspapers, magazines and TV and radio have forward planning departments or editors to pull in as much advance information about what is coming up in the news, and the PR world, so that they can plan stories and coverage.

giveaway A promotion, usually with the press, which involves free copies of a product being won by readers or given out if they call a hotline such as a freephone number.

green room The hospitality room in a TV or radio studio for guests, usually complete with coffee and nibbles, as well as TV monitors or speakers.

hook Same as an angle.

Hollis The bible of the PR industry, *Hollis Press & Public Relations Annual* lists news, research and PR contacts in major companies and consultancies.

hotline A telephone number which is released to the public, either for a promotion, or as part of crisis management, particularly in an emergency.

house style The written style of a company or consultancy that reflects the corporate identity.

image What PR is all about – making it, changing it or keeping it, and, above all, communicating it.

IPR Institute of Public Relations, Europe's largest trade organization for professionals in public relations. They run courses and awards, and have specialist groups on areas like finance, property and one for student members.

ISDN A form of technology that allows down-the-line (*q.v.*) interviews to be conducted by digital technology rather than by telephone wires; ISDN interviews are preferred by radio stations because they offer greater flexibility.

item A story or feature on TV or radio, within an overall programme.

launch Introducing a product, idea, person or campaign to attract publicity, that is, media coverage. Can involve anything from a news conference to a photocall.

lead-time Amount of time before a newspaper or magazine goes to press, or a TV or radio programme is broadcast or edited.

leader Column in a national newspaper, unsigned, which communicates the opinion of the newspaper on a subject to its readers.

listings Listings appear in every newspaper and local entertainment magazine and mention forthcoming events such as exhibitions, or openings of films, as well as TV and radio programmes.

lobby The lobby refers to the space in which MPs and peers converge during voting at Westminster. Lobby correspondents are expected to get unofficial gossip and unattributable briefings on 'what's really happening', unlike parliamentary journalists who record what actually happens in Parliament.

lobbyist A term for a professional in public affairs, whose job is to inform and influence to their or their clients' way of thinking politicians and those with power. Groups that lobby range from nurses to charities like Shelter for homeless people.

marketing mix Using the range of communication tools that advertising and PR offer, as well as traditional marketing, is described as the marketing mix.

market research Another word for opinion polls. Used by everyone from political parties to product managers to test out their ideas and products before they launch them – or afterwards if things don't go according to plan.

MPR The abbreviation for Marketing Public Relations, a relatively new American term which is about combining traditional marketing skills of focus on the product itself with PR techniques of talking about and generating interest in a product. A typical MPR campaign will combine a promotion with editorial coverage, and a giveaway of the product, or use of product placement.

mass media Mass media like TV or cinema reach huge audiences, rather than individual press or programmes aimed at specific audiences.

media monitoring Ways of tracking media coverage, or changes in the media itself, done either by companies or by individual PR departments or consultancies.

media relations Establishing and maintaining contact with journalists.

media schedule Produced for a launch or tour, detailing times, places for media appearances, interviews, photocalls, etc.

media training Preparation for the cameras, microphones or press interviews, often involves 'simulated' interviews – making people practise for the actual interview in a real TV or radio studio.

network Creating and nurturing contacts is networking.

news agency News editors in the press and on TV and radio either get their stories from their own correspondents or via news agencies such as Reuters or the Press Association (PA), who syndicate stories filed by their own journalists.

newsletter A communication tool often used by large companies to convey messages to staff or to customers.

no comment A formal way of avoiding answering a journalist's question.

on/off the record On the record means that the person giving the information knows that they may be quoted and the information directly used. Off the record means that the journalist cannot name the person or directly attribute the source of information.

op-ed Feature space in newspapers opposite the editorial or leader article.

on-line services Computer services ranging from media databases to press coverage archives from international systems like NEXUS and FT Profile.

peg Another word for hook or angle for a journalist.

photocall Photocalls or photo-opportunities aim to convey a message through pictures – still press pictures or moving TV pictures, either on their own or in addition to an event or press conference.

pitch PR consultancies prepare presentations to potential clients for new business. You can also pitch a story to journalists.

place Placing a story is another way of pitching or selling the idea of a story to a journalist.

plug 'Plug' or 'puff' are slang to describe the media coverage given to PR-led products or projects. Authors are often mocked for 'plugging' their latest book on TV and radio chat-shows.

public affairs The type of PR that deals with raising awareness about issues and campaigns to government, ministers and the civil service to change legislation.

PR Let's not forget that PR is the abbreviation for Public Relations.

PRCA Public Relations Consultants' Association, represents PR consultancies in the UK.

press cuttings Media coverage in the press is compiled either by the PR department or consultancy or by specialist agencies like Romeike and Curtis, and Durrants.

press conference A meeting called for TV, radio and press and organized by a company or consultancy to promote a launch, a news story or a person.

press kit   Pack containing relevant information for the media and other audiences.

press release   A brief summary of the message you are communicating sent to news editors and journalists with relevant information and contact numbers.

press officer   Generally means a PRO who deals with the media; another term for someone who handles media relations, but also involves other aspects of PR such as organization and briefings.

print media   Newspapers and magazines.

product placement   Getting a product such as a book shown in a TV show like *Brookside* is product placement, although the ITC (Independent Television Commission) guidelines are quite specific on this to distinguish it from advertising.

producer   The TV or radio journalist who puts together a programme, story or item.

promotion   A competition or marketing-led initiative, often a reader offer or giveaway.

PRO   Abbreviation of press officer, more accurate to use than to say 'PR' if you mean a person in public relations.

public   The public in public relations – ranges from the general public to customers, clients, shareholders, fellow professionals or the media.

publicity   Media coverage and public awareness as a result of PR

publicist   PRO who specializes in getting media coverage only.

Q & A   Questions and answers for the media, usually anticipated in advance by the PRO for their boss, spokesperson or client.

quote   A phrase said by a spokeswoman or client and offered to the media or quoted by them.

reader offer   A way of promoting a product through a newspaper or magazine.

retainer   A regular monthly payment instead of or together with fees paid to PR consultancies or freelance PROs.

ring-round   Telephone follow-up to the media to secure coverage or monitor interest.

satellite tour   Less common in the UK than in America, involving interviews with different TV and radio stations around the country or the world conducted through satellite links from one studio.

stringer   A journalist posted in a particular place who files copy back to their editor or producer.

snapper   Another word for photographer, more common now than *paparazzo*.

snowball effect   When a story takes off and 'runs' by itself.

sound-bite   A succinct quote, designed to be ready to use without editing.

spin   PRs putting their case to journalists, particularly in politics, has come to be known as spin, and political PROs in particular as 'spin doctors'.

sponsorship   A company pays to be associated with an event, launch or campaign, not directly advertising but having a more involved personal association.

story   Journalist's jargon for information which either is – or can lead to – an article or 'story'.

target audience   A term used in PR, advertising and marketing that describes who you are aiming at. Another word for the 'public' in public relations.

terrestrial TV   BBC 1 and 2, ITV and Channel 4 are terrestrial – land-based – TV channels.

tie-in   When a PR initiative links in with another event or with a particular medium like a newspaper.

transparency   A form of artwork of a photograph which can be easily reproduced in magazines. newspapers or for TV.

visual   Any kind of artwork provided to illustrate a story or campaign.

VNR   Means Video News Release, and it is prepared for companies or PR consultancies by professional TV journalists working for VNR agencies, who then edit the story and offer it to TV news programmes, ready-made.

website   A space on the Internet where products can be advertised or featured.

wires   A term to describe news agencies who send copy to newspapers 'down the wires'.

Advertising

ABC Short for Audit Bureau of Circulation. A publication's ABC figure is its independently audited circulation – that is, the number of people who buy it or to whom it is sent.

above-the-line Advertising is said to be above-the-line. Other lower profile marketing disciplines such as PR and sales promotion are said to be below-the-line.

Adshel Bus shelter poster site.

advertising research Research into the effectiveness of an advertising campaign or single advertisement.

BARB Broadcasters Audience Research Board. BARB produces viewing data for television programmes. It is the leading source of television audience research in the UK.

brand The name under which a product is marketed. Branded products are generally better known than the names of the companies that produce them. The most successful brands are associated in the mind's eye with their own clearly defined set of images and values. Examples of top brands are Coca-Cola, Persil, Reebok, Kleenex and, of course, *Cosmopolitan*.

broadsheet Large-format newspaper like the *Guardian*, *Times*, *Observer*, *Daily Telegraph* and *Independent*.

CAVIAR Cinema and Video Industry Audience Research.

classified Ads grouped together by category such as the recruitment, personal and commercial ads, etc., that appear in newspapers and magazines. Some publications, for example, *Loot* and *Exchange & Mart*, are devoted almost entirely to classified ads.

consumer durables Long-lasting, high-priced consumer products. Mainly household appliances, which can be divided into 'white goods' such as washing machines, fridges and freezers, and 'brown goods', such as TVs and music systems.

contract publishing Magazines produced by a publisher on behalf of a client. In recent years there has been a boom in this sector, which is worth about £100 million, with a growing number of companies bringing out magazines for their customers. *M&S Magazine* is a good example.

copy 1) The text of an ad. 2) A finished ad sent to a newspaper or magazine for publication.

copy instruction (CI) A form giving instructions to a publication about which ad should run in which position and on what date.

copywriting Writing the words of an ad.

CPT Cost Per Thousand. A term used when analysing the cost effectiveness of a medium at reaching consumers in a specific target group.

demographic class Advertisers sometimes target consumers by defining households as belonging to socio-economic classes A–E, based on the occupation of their main wage-earner. When advertisers talk about reaching ABC1s they mean the most affluent members of the population.

direct mail Advertising material sent directly to named individuals at their home or place of work.

direct marketing Marketing and supplying products directly to the consumer.

direct response Advertising containing a phone number or address that people can contact to get further information or to place an order.

display Whereas classified ads are predominantly text, usually positioned at the back of a publication, display ads are carefully designed and may include photography, illustrations and a range of typefaces. The glossy perfume, car and fashion ads in *Cosmo* are examples of display advertising.

double page spread (DPS) An ad running across two facing pages.

FMCG Fast-moving consumer goods. Products such as soap powders, tinned foods, bottled and canned drinks, etc., that sell in large quantities.

focus group A small, targeted group assembled for qualitative research purposes.

freesheet Free newspaper.

full service agency An ad agency that offers its clients services beyond the core functions like creative and media. These might include PR, sales promotion, packaging, etc.

gatefold A print ad that folds out.

infomercial an advertorial for the broadcast media.

JICREG Joint Industry Committee for Regional Press Research.

logo A company or brand's trademark design.

media pack An information pack sent by publishers to advertisers giving details about a publication's circulation figures, target market and advertising rates, etc.

medium Singular of media.

moderator The person, usually an employee of a market research company, who questions and guides a focus group.

NRS National Readership Survey. Measures the average readership per issue of newspapers and consumer magazines. Also analyses the frequency and quality of reading.

OSCAR Outside Site Classification & Audience Research. The research system that provided audience data on the 120,000-plus roadside panels owned by members of the Outdoor Advertising Association. It was replaced in Spring 1996 by Postar.

OTS Opportunity To See. Average number of times an ad is seen by the target audience of a medium.

outdoor The collective term for the poster and transport media.

portfolio Examples of a creative team's or photographer/illustrator's work. Known colloquially as their 'book'.

Postar Poster Audience Research. The new audience research system for outdoor media which superseded OSCAR in Spring 1996.

repro house Short for reproduction house and sometimes called a colour house. The repro house is where type and pictures are converted into four-colour film for printing.

qualitative research Research using small samples (for example, focus group discussions or one-to-one interviews) to find out people's attitudes, opinions and impressions.

quantitative research Large, statistically valid pieces of market research, for instance, asking a representative sample of 1,000 people whether they have heard of a particular soft drink. The results are expressed numerically: for example, 85 per cent said they had heard of Irn Bru.

RAJAR Radio Joint Audience Research, the radio equivalent of BARB. It measures audience listening figures for BBC and commercial radio stations.

ratecard A price-list for advertising space.

readership The readers of a publication. A title's readership is higher than its circulation because a single issue is often read by more than one person.

showreel Examples of any agency or independent production company's TV/film work.

strapline The slogan, for example, 'To Be This Good Takes Sega' or 'Probably the Best Lager in the World'.

tabloid Compact format newspaper like the *Mirror* or *Mail*.

TGI Target Group Index. A continuous survey of UK consumers widely used by advertisers, advertising agencies and media owners to shape marketing strategy and plan campaigns. TGI is carried out by market research company BMRB International.

tracking Following the awareness generated by, and effectiveness of, a particular advertising campaign.

traffic The ad agency department that progresses creative jobs.

Chapter 11 / **Getting a Job**

How to Handle the Job Hunt

Finding a job is always hard work, and as jobs in PR and advertising are more coveted than most, trying to land one is not for the faint of heart. You need vast reserves of resilience, persistence and determination. Even the most junior role may attract hundreds of applicants so it could take some time, and a few rejections, before you finally strike it lucky.

First Steps

It's important to have a clear idea of which aspect of PR or advertising will best suit you, so research the subject and read books about the media to find out which job areas appeal.

The best way to find out what a particular job is really like is to talk to people who do it, so call people in your target area and ask if they would be prepared to chat to you for fifteen to twenty minutes about their work. The worst they can do is say no, but you may be pleasantly surprised by the number of people who'll be happy to spare you some time. Make it clear that you're just looking for information and are not expecting to be offered a job. As well as asking them what their work involves, you could sound them out about the state of the industry, trends in the way things are going or what employers look for. Don't abuse their generosity – if you asked for fifteen minutes of their time, try not to take up more, unless they're obviously happy to carry on – and remember to send a thank-you letter soon after.

If your research reveals obvious gaps in your training or

knowledge, do something about it, whether it's enrolling on a word-processing course or attending an industry conference. As well as improving your skills base, you'll also be providing an employer with a positive demonstration of your commitment and enthusiasm. Make sure you *know* about the industry. Read the specialist press and the media pages of the newspapers (see p. 159) so that you're up to date on the issues affecting it. That way, you'll also know when companies are expanding or have won new business and might therefore be looking to recruit more staff.

If you're a student planning to break in after you leave university, you need to start gathering skills, practical experience and training as soon as possible to give you the edge over all the other thousands of graduates who'll be chasing jobs and postgraduate courses in the same narrow field. As well as the obvious things like getting involved on the student newspaper or campus radio, make the most of any free training on offer, in computing or languages, for example, all of which can be useful skills in advertising and PR.

The one thing that counts more than anything is relevant work experience. The more you have the better, so good vacation jobs are vital. If you have secretarial skills, you may be able to find temping work. The other way of getting that all-important experience – and real insider view – is by offering to work for free. A good placement will teach you more about the job than any careers book or counsellor can and the experience gained can be more valuable than all the paper qualifications in the world when it comes to getting a permanent job. It's also a chance to make useful contacts and, if it goes well, will stand you in good stead when vacancies come up. You're unlikely to be paid but some companies will cover your expenses – look on it as an investment.

Making the most of work experience

- Lots of students look for work experience in the holidays, so you're more likely to get in if you can work during term-time. Apply at least a couple of months in advance of when you want to start as it can be difficult to find a place.
- Be reliable. Even though you're not getting paid a fortune – if you're paid at all – you should behave professionally, arriving on time and not leaving before the end of the working day.
- Most of the work you're given will be thoroughly mundane (would *you* trust an inexperienced student with anything else?), but if you do the photocopying and tea-making with good grace you'll make a good impression. Do it with enthusiasm – offer before being asked – and you'll definitely be remembered. However boring the tasks, do them all *well*: every little detail matters.
- It's always better to ask questions if you're doing something you don't understand than to blunder ahead and get it wrong. But whenever you ask a question, pay attention to the answer and write everything down so you don't irritate people by asking the same things over and over again.
- Remember people's names: draw a plan of the office with names by desks to jog your memory.
- Try to move around departments to get a flavour of each, rather than staying at one desk the whole time.
- How you handle people on the phone will be noticed, so be polite, try to sound authoritative and make sure when you take messages that you get the contact's name and number and note down the date and time. Watch how other people deal with callers for hints on how to behave. Don't take the opportunity of the 'free' phones to call all your friends – if you must make a personal call, ask permission first.
- Use your initiative. If someone looks really busy, offer to help; if the phone rings at an empty desk, answer it. Ask if there's any outstanding filing you could do or if the bookshelves need

tidying. If there's really nothing, use the time to practise on the computer.
- If the placement was successful, ask someone you worked closely with if they would provide a reference for you. Try to get them to do it before you leave, or very soon after, before they forget who you are. If there's anyone you get on with particularly well, stay in contact and let them know you'd love to hear when any jobs are going.

Finding a Job

The tabloid *Media* section of Monday's *Guardian* is by far and away the best of the national newspapers for jobs in PR and media sales and, less frequently, advertising. You should make sure you read it every week. It's also worth trying *The Times* on Wednesdays (media, sales and marketing jobs, but mostly the latter) and the *Independent* on Tuesdays. The *Daily Mail* and *Daily Telegraph* both have recruitment advertising sections on Thursdays, which may sometimes have suitable jobs. London's *Evening Standard* has a media section on Wednesdays, which is a good source of media sales vacancies. Those looking to come into PR or advertising via the secretarial route should head for La Crème de la Crème in *The Times* on Mondays, Wednesdays and Thursdays.

You should also look for jobs in the following trade publications:

Broadcast Published weekly by Emap Media, costs £1.90. Subscription: 0171 505 8119. Occasionally has broadcast media sales jobs.

Campaign Carries ads for jobs in advertising, media sales/buying and marketing, published weekly by Haymarket Business Publications, costs £2.00. Subscription: 0181 845 8545.

Marketing Published weekly by Haymarket Business Publications, costs £1.90. Subscriptions: 0181 845 8545. Excellent source of marketing vacancies.

Marketing Week Published weekly by Centaur Communications, costs £1.90. Subscriptions: 0171 292 3711. Good source of marketing jobs.

Media Week Carries ads for media sales and buying jobs, published weekly by Emap Media, costs £1.85. Subscriptions: 0181 956 3016. Emap also has an Internet site which advertises media jobs: www.emap.co.uk/media/

PR Week Carries ads for PR jobs, published weekly by Haymarket Business Publications, costs £1.70. Subscription: 0181 845 8545.

When you see a job ad that interests you, study it carefully. What sort of qualities and experience do you think the interviewer is looking for? How can you demonstrate that you have them? Don't be afraid to apply for a job if you don't have every single quality asked for in the ad – employers know that the perfect candidate is a rare bird. As long as you meet *most* of the requirements, you're in with a chance.

However, sitting back and waiting for the perfect ad to appear in the paper could take years – so don't. Go out looking instead. It's been estimated that only 10 per cent of people find jobs by answering newspaper ads and many employers try to cut costs and avoid a deluge of applications by relying on word-of-mouth to find suitable candidates. This definitely holds true in PR and advertising, where employers receive so many on-spec applications or word-of-mouth recommendations that they rarely need to advertise jobs, especially at junior level. Write directly to the person in charge of the department you want to work in, rather than to Personnel, and specify the kind of work you're looking for. Your letter may then be passed on to Personnel but not before it's been seen by the person who makes the decisions about who to employ.

Networking is one of the best ways of finding a job so increase your visibility and experience by attending relevant courses or industry conferences or talks. If anyone you know is employed in a company for which you want to work, ask them to keep an ear to the ground and an eye on the in-house noticeboards and magazines to find out if any jobs are going. Some companies offer a cash incentive to employees who can introduce new staff to the company and save them advertising.

Get in touch with the specialist PR and advertising recruitment consultancies. Although they are mostly asked to find experienced candidates for their clients they sometimes have more junior vacancies on their books. Even if they haven't they can be a useful source of information about which companies may be recruiting in the near future and the kind of vacancies they are likely to have. Once again, be courteous and succinct: recruitment consultants are often happy to spare a few minutes to give some free advice but most are extremely busy and won't appreciate you wasting their time. Here's a list of recruitment consultants broken down by their areas of specialization.

Advertising Agencies

Account handling and planning

Wendy Braverman Associates
8 Ryders Terrace, London NW8 0EE
Telephone: 0171 372 1575

Haigh Recruitment Consultants
12–14 Bristol Gardens, Little Venice,
London W9 2JG
Telephone: 0171 286 2827

The Headhunters Partnership
40 Hanway Street, London W1P 9DE
Telephone: 0171 631 4224

Creative and account handling

Harold MacGregor
83 George Street, London W1H 5PL
Telephone: 0171 486 2773

Kendall Tarrant
83 Charlotte Street, London W1P 1LB
Telephone: 0171 636 1633

Creative services, creative and account handling

Terry Grant Associates
Midford Place, 114/115 Tottenham
Court Road, London W1P 9HL
Telephone 0171 388 8080

Advertising on the client side

Ball & Hoolahan
First Floor, 75–77 Margaret Street,
London W1N 7HB
Telephone: 0171 323 4041

The Lloyd Group
Alhambra House, 27–31 Charing Cross Road, London WC2H 0AU
Telephone: 0171 930 5161

Michael Page Marketing
Page House, 39–41 Parker Street,
London WC2H 5LH
Telephone: 0171 831 2000.
(Also branches in Birmingham, 0121 233 4633; Leeds, 0113 2423530; Eton, Berkshire, 01753 833752.)

Media

Most of the following specialize in media sales. The Stevens Company is a broadcast specialist that recruits for both media buyers and media owners.

Carreras Lathane Associates
4 Golden Square, London W1R 3AE
Telephone: 0171 439 9634

The Davis Company
32/34 Great Titchfield Street, London W1P 7AD
Telephone: 0171 580 4580

Graduate Recruitment Company
(A division of Phee Farrer Jones),
20 Piccadilly, London W1V 9PF
Telephone: 0171 734 2228

Hills Flower Strong
Glen House, 200/208 Tottenham Court Road, London W1P 9LA
Telephone: 0171 323 4770

Lipton Fleming
18/19 Bentinck Street, London
W1M 5RL
Telephone: 0171 486 4419

Media Appointments
7A Langley Street, London
WC2H 9JA
Telephone: 0171 379 0333

Media Contacts
The Windsor Centre, Windsor Street, Islington, London N1 8QG
Telephone: 0171 359 8244

The Media Exchange
26–28 Great Portland Street, London
W1N 5AD
Telephone: 0171 636 6777

Moriati Media
Premier House, 77 Oxford Street,
London W1R 1RB
Telephone: 0171 439 1188/434 3960

Price Jamieson
Paramount House, 104–108 Oxford
Street, London W1N 9FA
Telephone: 0171 631 1005
Advertises some jobs on the Internet:
http://www.gold.net/PriceJam/

The Stevens Company
Regent House, Fourth Floor, 235–241
Regent Street, London W1R 7AG
Telephone: 0171 629 2939

PR

Executive Creative & Media
Pear Tree Farm, Wigmore,
Herefordshire HR6 9UR
Telephone: 01568 770732

The Grapevine
13 Croft Road, Wilmslow, Cheshire
SK9 6JJ
Telephone: 01625 525833

Media Appointments
(see above)

Tessa Dorcey Associates
207 Regent Street, London W1R 7DD
Telephone: 0171 287 5091

Judy Farquharson Ltd
47 New Bond Street, London
W1Y 9HA
Telephone: 0171 493 8824

Graduate Appointments
(see p. 134)

Vicky Mann & Associates
39 Bedford Square, London
WC1B 3EG
Telephone: 0171 436 4243

The Lloyd Group
(see p. 162)

Peter Childs Associates
38 South Molten Street, London
W1Y 1HA
Telephone: 0171 495 3930

Taylor Bennett
Management Placement, Suite 8 De
Walden Court, 85 New Cavendish
Street, London W1M 7RA
Telephone: 0171 580 4300

Price Jamieson Group
(see above)

The Perfect CV

The purpose of a CV is to get you an interview – and that applies whether you're writing to an employer on spec or applying for an advertised vacancy. The idea is to make it a tempting taster so that they'll want to find out more. It's not meant to tell the whole story of your life and should never be more than two sides long – no employer is going to want to read more than that. For recent graduates, one page is enough. Tailor your CV to each different job you apply for, emphasizing or downplaying different aspects as relevant. The fact that you spent several vacations working in catering may be of limited interest if you're applying for a job as an ad agency designer, but if you're being interviewed for an in-house PR job at a large hotel chain it could provide relevant experience and knowledge of the industry. Remember to adapt your CV as the years go on, adding, cutting and rewriting. For example, the further away you get from your schooldays, the less relevant your O levels and GCSEs become, so prune back the details as more relevant experience supersedes them. Nor do you need to carry on putting down the holiday job you did when you were sixteen.

There are many different styles of CV and it's largely a question of taste as to which you choose. The traditional and most widely recognized CV is one that follows a chronological format. After your basic personal details – name, address, telephone number; date of birth, nationality – give your career history, starting with your current or most recent job first, and working backwards. State the job title, company name, period of employment, give a brief job description and mention any special achievements. Describe your current job in most detail; be more succinct about any before that. After Career History, list Educational Qualifications, again working backwards. You may also wish to include Other Information, such as driving licence, foreign languages, computer skills.

Alternatively, you could opt for a functional or skills CV. It's not as common but is useful if you have had frequent job changes, if you are trying to change career direction or if you have a limited career history but have acquired relevant skills and experience in other areas, such as voluntary work or work experience. It also takes the emphasis off any gaps. Under headings such as Communications Experience, Administrative Abilities or Communications Skills, summarize your experience in those areas. If you're applying for an advertised job, make sure you match your headings to the qualities asked for in the ad. Voluntary work is a good source of transferable skills: teaching adult literacy or English as a second language calls for effective communication skills and an ability to motivate others; editing the student newspaper will probably have brought you experience in editing, writing, researching and design.

Your third option is a targeted CV, best used when you're applying for jobs on spec rather than in response to specific job advertisements. The emphasis is on aiming for a specific position and explaining why you're qualified for it. Under the heading 'Job Target' state the position you're aiming for. Then, under headings such as 'Capabilities' and 'Achievements', list your skills and talents which relate to your prospective position, and detail what you've done so far that shows you'd be able to perform in the job. Further headings should include 'Work Experience' and 'Education', as on a chronological CV.

Whichever format you choose, there are certain basic rules to follow:

- Use good quality white or off-white paper. Avoid anything fancy or gimmicky.
- Make the layout as attractive and accessible as possible: use a clear, easy-to-read typeface and leave wide margins and spaces between sections.
- Avoid long sentences. An employer wants to see the key facts at a glance and won't be impressed by rambling prose. Keep phrases short, punchy and active, starting with a verb, e.g. 'developed new campaign', 'improved copy flow system'. You don't need to

say 'I' every time – who else would you be talking about in your CV?

- Cut out anything inessential. You don't need to include addresses of employers or educational institutions. If you have a degree it's not necessary to itemize every GCSE subject and grade.
- A CV should always be typed – and *well* typed. If you can't do it yourself or don't have access to a machine, get someone who can and does to do it for you.
- There's no need to include referees here unless you have such stunningly good ones that it would impress an employer. Never give anyone's name as a referee without checking with them first.
- Check, double-check and triple-check your CV, then give it to a friend to check again. Any mistakes will count against you.
- Eliminate the negative. A CV is a selling document, not the place to advertise every exam you've ever failed or career setback you've faced.
- Don't include current salary details unless asked to do so. People will make certain assumptions about you and your worth if you give them specific figures and you could put yourself out of the running by earning too little or too much. Plenty of time to talk money later.
- Include interests and hobbies if you have little work experience as yet; otherwise, leave them out unless they demonstrate a skill or quality relevant to the job or are so unusual that they will intrigue the interviewer.
- If applying for jobs abroad, enclose a passport photograph of yourself – it's far more common to do this in other European countries than it is here.
- If you're responding to a job advertisement, make sure that the skills you highlight in your CV match those specified in the ad.
- Extra skills such as computer literacy and foreign languages are valuable, but don't make them up to impress. If you claim to have fluent French, for example, you could find an interviewer asking you some questions in that language.

Positive/active words that stand out on CVs

achieved • administered • analysed • built • capable
communicated • competent • consistent • controlled
co-ordinated • created • designed • developed • directed
economical • edited • effective • efficient • established
expanded • experienced • guided • implemented • improved
increased • initiated • introduced • led • managed
monitored • organized • participated • positive • processed
produced • professional • proficient • profitable • qualified
repaired • researched • resourceful • responsible • skilled
sold • specialized • stable • successful • supervised • trained
versatile • volunteered • wrote

The Covering Letter

Never send off a CV or application form without a covering letter – you'll miss a great opportunity to sell yourself. (If you have a glowing testimonial or letter of recommendation from a former employer, you could enclose that too.) Keep it short and to the point: it should fit on to one sheet, preferably on the same, high-quality paper as your CV.

Put your address in the top right-hand corner or centred at the top of the page, with the date and address of the person you're sending it to below that on the left-hand side. Make sure you address the letter to someone by name rather than 'the Personnel Officer' or 'Dear Sir/Madam'. Call the company first to find out, and always check the spelling. The correct ending to a letter addressed to a person by name is 'Yours sincerely'. 'Yours faithfully' is only used when the addressee is Dear Sir or Dear Madam.

Make sure the letter is tidy: if there are lots of applicants for a job, it's easy to start by discarding the ones whose replies are scruffy or ill-prepared. Typing looks smarter, unless the employer specifically requests a hand-written letter, in which case draft it on a rough piece of paper first, so that you can produce the final copy without mistakes. Use blue or (preferably) black ink; other colours are generally frowned upon and green ink is considered the trademark of a loony.

With any job application, it's important that your spelling, grammar and punctuation are correct; if you're applying for a job in media relations, it's *doubly* important. If you're applying for a specific job, say how you heard about it and if there is a reference number, include it. And if you're writing at the suggestion of someone the employer knows personally or someone who is well known in the field, then mention it straightaway. Keep the language simple: many people make the mistake of using over-formal, flowery phrases, which just sound stilted and unnatural. State briefly why you are a strong candidate and emphasize what you have to offer the employer: 'As a member of the university debating team, I have had plenty of experience in marshalling an argument and communicating it persuasively.' It is not good enough to say, 'I'd love to work in advertising.' So would a million others. Draw attention to the relevant bits of your CV but don't go into details – save that for the interview.

Don't write a fabulous letter then ruin the effect by cramming it into a tiny little envelope. Your paper should never be folded more than twice, so make sure your envelope is A4, A5 or 220 x 110 mm.

Application Forms

Many companies, especially large organizations, ask all applicants to fill in an application form rather than sending in a CV. It makes it easier for them to find the information they need to know quickly, which is invaluable when dealing with large numbers of candidates.

Photocopy the blank form and do a rough version of your answers on the photocopy first, then once you're happy with it, copy them on to the original. Complete all sections, however irrelevant they might seem. Don't leave the Further Information box blank – it's a chance to say things you haven't had the opportunity to say elsewhere. Look back at the job ad to see what they were asking for and if you haven't had a chance to prove how well you match the description anywhere else, now's your chance. Write legibly and in black ink: the form will probably be photocopied and blue ink doesn't photocopy well.

Take a photocopy of the finished form as a useful reference for the next time you have to fill one in.

Interviews

Interviews can be nerve-racking, especially for first-time job-hunters – and the more you want the job, the worse it is. Nerves come, in a large part, from feeling unready and unprepared, so the more you plan ahead, the better your chances and the better you'll feel on the day. Research may be time-consuming but it's worth it: it shows initiative and motivation and will give you a great advantage over candidates who haven't bothered. If you're ignorant about the company's work, then you're obviously not that interested in them or, presumably, the job. Don't be careless: confusing the company's clients or products with those of a rival won't win you any friends.

You should already be reading the relevant trade press (see pp. 181–3) to keep up to date on the industry generally. Whatever the job you're going for, the following tips apply.

- Expect to be asked about your personal life and leisure interests as well as strictly work issues. The employer is trying to put together a picture of you as a complete person.
- If you're working already, prepare a clear, succinct précis of your job and be prepared to answer questions on any aspect of it. Past performance is the main thing employers have to rely on when it comes to assessing how well you would do with them, so make sure you feed them relevant examples of past experience.

How have you shown initiative, reliability, creativity, organizational flair, etc.? Can you work well under pressure or adapt to changing conditions? What computer systems can you use?

- Be ready to explain why you're interested in this job. Sounds obvious, yes, but it's surprising how many people don't think it through.
- Be prepared for tests. You might, for example, be asked to pick out the mistakes in a deliberately error-strewn press release.
- Straightforward questions about your studies, qualifications or job history are relatively easy to answer and you should certainly expect to be asked any of the questions in the box. Many media interviews are relatively informal chats but there are always some interviewers who like to spring on you horrors such as 'How would your best friend/worst enemy/colleagues describe you?' or 'What are your strengths/weaknesses?' You're unlikely to think of something suitable on the spot so it helps to have examples prepared. *Great Answers to Tough Interview Questions*, Martin John Yate (Kogan Page £6.99), has some great tips on how to answer tricky ones.

Questions You're Likely to be Asked

Tell me about yourself.
What makes you right for this job?
Why do you want to work for us?
What do you like/dislike in your current job?
Why do you want to leave your current job?
Where do you see yourself in five years' time?
Tell me all about your current job.
What computer systems have you worked on?
How do you feel about working long hours?

- If you're going for your first job after school or university, you're unlikely to have much work experience, so you'll have to look to other areas for skills and experience to offer employers. Did you participate in team sports? Write for the school magazine? Make short films with the film society? Take leading roles in school plays? Serve on a hall-of-residence committee? Deliver seminars? Undertake extensive or unusual travel during vacations? Have you done voluntary work, served time on a local community committee or been involved in an advisory board? What about work placements during vacations? Be prepared to answer questions about why you did these things and what you feel you've gained from them. Even things that seem irrelevant to you may help to give an employer a fuller picture of you.

• As much as anything, they want evidence that you are reliable and responsible so even non-advertising and PR-related work experience at weekends or in vacations could illustrate those qualities. If you've paid for any postgraduate studies yourself, it shows strong motivation and commitment so make sure you mention it. If you're a bit rusty at interviews try to run the whole thing through with a more practised friend beforehand, getting her to play the interviewer – she may come up with more possible questions you hadn't thought of. You may feel silly at first but it *will* help. Ask for honest feedback and don't get upset or defensive if there are negative points, as that will discourage further comment. Don't over-rehearse or you'll end up sounding stilted and unnatural when you want to appear spontaneous and relaxed.

• You don't always get much notice of an interview so don't leave all your preparation until the letter arrives: start thinking about it when you do your application.

• Don't spend so long worrying about the questions you'll be asked that you forget the basics. Get plenty of sleep the night before the interview. Work out in advance how you're going to get there and how long it will take – and allow extra time for delays. Make sure a couple of days ahead that your clothes are clean and ready.

On the Day

Getting in the Mood

- Be positive! If you've been asked for an interview, they're obviously interested in you. To get to this stage you've probably already beaten hundreds of others and may be on a shortlist of between six and twelve. The employer already believes you are *capable* of the job; all you have to do is prove it.
- Do anything to help boost your confidence: read a favourite poem or inspirational book on the way to the interview, listen to 'up' music on your Walkman, remind yourself of all the times you've triumphed against the odds or all the things you've done that make you feel proud.
- Reread your letter/CV/application form and be ready to answer questions on anything you've included. Take copies with you in case the interviewer has mislaid them.
- Take a spare pair of tights, needle and cotton – for emergency repairs – phonecard and small change – for parking or phone calls. Make sure you have the company's phone number so you can call in an emergency. And don't forget to take their address.
- Set out in plenty of time and aim to arrive ten to fifteen minutes early. Don't expect buses or trains to turn up on time or assume that you'll find a parking space easily. Use your waiting time to watch the people around you, read any internal noticeboards or in-house newsletters, and generally try to get a feel for the place.
- Don't smoke or drink shortly before the interview – smelling of smoke or alcohol isn't going to impress any interviewer.

Looking the Part

Don't underestimate the importance of appearance. Research has shown that an interviewer's impression of you will be made up of 55 per cent how you look, 38 per cent on how you sound and only 7 per cent on what you say. First impressions are quickly formed and hard to change, and although your interview might last an hour, a decision has probably been largely made within the first four or five minutes.

- Your clothes don't need to be expensive – nobody expects someone fresh out of college to waltz in in Armani – but they must be presentable and clean. Make sure they're comfortable, too: you can't concentrate if you're too busy worrying about wayward buttons or squirming around because your skirt's too tight.
- Dress appropriately for the organization: you wouldn't necessarily wear the same outfit for interviews at the Home Office and MTV. As a general rule, though, think smart rather than trendy. Some experts recommend going to watch staff leaving or entering the workplace to get an idea of the corporate image, and tailor your outfit accordingly (same kind of clothes but a bit smarter).
- Heels look smarter than flat – but not *too* high – and studies suggest that wearing light, natural make-up rather than none increases your chances of success by 20 per cent.
- Don't smoke, even if invited to do so – it looks messy. And unless you're ultra-relaxed refuse any offers of tea or coffee – it just provides more scope for disaster.
- Don't go into the interview room clutching carrier bags of shopping or a dripping wet coat and umbrella; leave any encumbrances with the receptionist.
- Try to appear confident, even if you're quaking inside. Walk in confidently and sit upright but relaxed in the chair. Leaning forward slightly shows attention and interest. Look the interviewer in the eye but don't fix her with an unwavering stare. Speak up and, if you tend to gabble when nervous, make a conscious effort to

speak more slowly. Try to sound enthusiastic. Keep your arms and legs uncrossed, don't shift around in your seat and try not to fiddle with jewellery or your hair. Merely sitting comfortably gives you the desired impression of calm and confidence.

- However nervous you feel, *smile*! Most interviewers base their final decisions on gut feeling, and it's only natural that they will warm more to someone who appears relaxed and friendly, who they think will be pleasant to work with as well as able to do the job.
- Don't save your best behaviour for the interviewer alone: be just as pleasant to the receptionist and anyone else with whom you make contact – they may be asked for their impressions.

In the Interview

- If the interviewer starts by asking you a few general questions, like how your journey to the interview was, they're only trying to put you at your ease. Don't go into great detail.
- A little humour or wit at appropriate moments will make you more memorable to an interviewer and provide a bit of light relief in what is possibly a rather dull day of grilling nervous candidates.
- Concentrate on listening properly to what the interviewer is saying rather than fretting about how you're doing and what she might ask next. If you miss something or are confused by a question, it's better to ask for clarification than to waffle on with an inappropriate answer. Keep your answers relevant.
- It's normal to play up your good points and try to skim over the bad ones. But you don't want to look as if you have something to hide, so if the interviewer does ask about any area you'd hoped to avoid – a previous redundancy, say, or a series of short-term jobs – answer briefly but honestly.
- If you're asked why you want to leave your current job, don't just say you're bored or hate your boss, even if it's true. Couch your reasons in more positive terms: 'I've learned a great deal in the job but now I've reached a stage where there are no immediate promotion prospects and I'm ready to tackle new challenges/take on more responsibility/use talents that are under-used.'

- Be specific in your answers. If you're asked how you would handle situation X, for example, if you can, say how you dealt successfully with a similar situation in the past.
- Employers usually take up references so don't lie about something a referee might be asked to corroborate.
- Panel or board interviews can be especially daunting but at least you're less at the whim of one person's likes and dislikes. Sit somewhere where you can see everyone and they can all see you – if the chair's in the wrong place, move it. Members of the panel usually take it in turns to ask questions and you should watch the questioner as she talks to you, then address your answers mainly to her, but include the other panel members with occasional eye contact. Return your gaze to the chairperson at the end. If possible, find out in advance who the members of the panel will be. Try to memorize the names and to be equally polite and friendly to all members whatever their manner. When you get your turn to ask questions, direct them to the chair, who can redirect them to the appropriate member of the panel.
- If there's a silence after you've given your answer to a question, don't feel you have to blunder in and fill it. Just ask the interviewer if you've made yourself clear and put the ball back in their court.
- If you're asked about your hobbies and interests, don't say anything you can't back up. If you say you're keen on the theatre, say, expect to be asked, 'What's the best play you've seen recently?'
- Remember, this is a two-way process: it's a time for you to find out about the potential employer and the job as well as vice versa, so don't miss your chance when asked if you have any questions. It also provides another opportunity for you to impress. Prepare three or four intelligent questions that demonstrate your genuine interest in the job or your familiarity with the business and the challenges facing it. Write them down on an index card if you think you might forget them and keep it conveniently to hand. If the interviewer doesn't offer you the chance to ask questions, then volunteer, but remember that asking too many is as bad as asking none at all. If all your questions have been answered during the course of the interview, then say so. Be sensitive about time and

alert to signs of impatience in the interviewer: remember that the next candidate is probably waiting.
- Questions about childcare and marital status are illegal but that doesn't stop some people asking them. If you want the job, it's probably best just to deal with them briefly but assure the interviewer that you can cope and wouldn't have applied for the job otherwise.
- Don't leave without asking how soon you can expect to hear from them.

Money Matters

Many people accept whatever money is offered in their relief at getting the job, but salary is almost always open to negotiation, providing you go about it in the right way.

Before you go to an interview, try to find out the going rate for the job. Ask people working in the industry; contact professional associations; look at similar job ads to see if they mention money. If you're asked how much you earn now, remember to take into account any perks you may have (subsidized canteen, pension, profit share, interest-free travel loan, medical insurance, etc.). Always try to get the employer to mention a figure before you do, but if they ask you to say what you're looking for, don't think in terms of what you need but in terms of what the job is worth. Don't give a fixed figure, but a range: 'I'm looking for something in the high twenties' or 'I would hope for a substantial increase on the £12,000 I'm earning now.' If they give a range, aim for the top.

If the employer is immovable on the money or won't go as high as you'd like, think about other areas that might be open to negotiation, such as flexible working hours, an early salary appraisal, training opportunities, a company car.

After the Interview

Assess your performance and see if there's anything you can learn from it. What went well? What went badly? If there were any questions that caught you out, brush up your answers for next time. If, despite all your best efforts, the interview was a disaster, don't automatically blame yourself. If you're unlucky enough to land an unpleasant or aggressive interviewer, you'll just have to write it off to experience and remind yourself that the next one can only be better.

However the interview went, it's a good idea to write the next day, thanking the interviewer for seeing you, reinforcing any important points and adding any extra relevant information you might have forgotten or been unable to pass on at the time. Keep it short and sweet – just enough to nudge the interviewer's memory and show that you really are keen. If you don't hear anything within the time expected, write or call to find out the state of play. Let them know if you have other interviews/offers to consider but don't make it sound like a threat. After the initial enquiry, leave it – hassling only irritates people.

If you're offered the job, clarify all terms and conditions before accepting. If you wait until you're in the job before sorting things out, you're in a weaker position to bargain. Don't hand in your notice in your current job until you have something in writing from your new employer: a verbal offer can be withdrawn.

If you don't get the job but you're still keen to work for the company, write and say you were sorry to be unsuccessful this time but would like to be kept on file in case of future vacancies. It wouldn't hurt to ask what the person who was appointed had that you didn't. Make it clear you're just looking for helpful feedback, and not demanding explanations. At least it might give you something useful to take away from the experience rather than seeing it as a total failure.

Keeping up morale is important. It can be discouraging when you apply unsuccessfully over and over again, especially when your friends are all finding their dream jobs, but don't let yourself sink into depression. Treat each interview as practice and remember that if you take great care over your letters and CVs you're already streets ahead of most people. Your time will come.

Chapter 12 / **Further Information**

Useful Addresses

Advertising Association
Abford House, 15 Wilton Road,
London SW1V 1NJ
Telephone: 0171 828 4831
The Advertising Association, a federation of trade associations representing advertisers, ad agencies and the media, has a library containing over 2,000 volumes on advertising, the media and marketing. The library is open free of charge to non-members between 2 p.m. and 4 p.m. Tuesdays to Fridays. Space is limited so it is important to make an appointment with one of the Association's information officers.

Advertising Film & Video Tape Producers Association
26 Noel Street, London W1V 3RD
Telephone: 0171 434 2651

The Adwomen
c/o Margaret Frewer, UK Poster Sales, 7A High Road, Chadwell Heath, Essex RM6 6PU
Telephone: 0181 597 9304
A networking body for women working in advertising. Membership costs £15 a year.

Association of Media & Communications Specialists (AMCO)
163 Rickmansworth High Street, Hertfordshire WD3 1AY
Telephone: 01923 711981
Represents companies in fields such as media buying and market research who have an interest in communication through media. Able to act as an informal clearing house by passing CVs on to its members.

The Cable Communications Association
Fifth Floor, Artillery House, Artillery Row, London SW1P 1RT
Telephone: 0171 255 3000
Can supply general information on the cable TV sector. Also runs a hotline which you can call to find out details about your local cable company. The number is 0990 111777.

CAM Foundation
The Communication Advertising & Marketing Foundation, Abford House, 15 Wilton Road, London SW1V 1NJ
Telephone: 0171 828 7506
Can supply a prospectus and a leaflet on NVQs in advertising, public relations, direct marketing and sales promotion.

The Chartered Institute of Marketing
Moor Hall, Cookham, Maidenhead, Berkshire SL6 9QH
Telephone: 01628 852173
The leading marketing organization in Europe, with over 50,000 members. Its student registration officer can give advice on careers and qualifications in marketing. Members of the Institute have access to its library and marketing information centre INFOMARK.

The Cinema Advertising Association
127 Wardour Street, London W1V 4AD Telephone: 0171 439 9531
The trade association for cinema advertising contractors. It produces an annual factsheet.

Creative Circle
22 Poland Street, London W1V 3DD
Telephone: 0171 734 9334
Runs the 'First' competitions which are open free of charge to students at art college. Entrants are given a creative brief, usually for a charity. Anyone who makes it through to the final stages stands a high chance of getting work in advertising.

The Designers & Art Directors Association (D&AD)
Graphite Square, 85 Vauxhall Walk, London SE11 5HJ
Telephone: 0171 582 6487
Runs the highly regarded creative concept workshops. It also runs advertising's equivalent of the Oscars: the D&AD creative awards are the biggest advertising awards of their kind in the world with 15,000 entries every year.

Direct Marketing Association
Haymarket House, 1 Oxendon Street, London SW1Y 4EE
Telephone: 0171 321 2525
Can supply information on member companies that run graduate-training schemes and those looking to recruit graduates. Also able to provide statistics on the size of the direct-marketing industry.

The History of Advertising Trust
Unit 6, The Raveningham Centre, Raveningham, Norwich NR14 6NU
Telephone: 01508 548623
A charity that runs what may be the world's largest advertising archives containing about 2 million items, including print, television and radio ads, advertising proofs, and artwork, storyboards and research material. The library is open to students by prior appointment at a cost of £12.50 per day; those already working in advertising have to pay substantially more. The Trust will try to answer any postal queries about past advertising as long as you send them a stamped, self-addressed envelope.

Incorporated Society of British Advertisers
44 Hertford Street, London W1Y 8AE
Telephone: 0171 499 7502
ISBA represents over 1,000 UK advertisers.

Institute of Direct Marketing
1 Park Road, Teddington, Middlesex TW11 0AR
Telephone: 0181 977 5705
Can supply information on direct marketing.

Institute of Practitioners in Advertising
44 Belgrave Square, London
SW1X 8QS
Telephone: 0171 235 7020
The body that represents advertising agencies. It has produced a video and brochure on advertising, available in careers offices.

Institute of Public Relations (IPR)
The Old Trading House, 15 Northburgh Street, London
EC1V OPR
Telephone: 0171 253 5151
Europe's largest public-relations trade organization for individuals in public relations, the IPR has over 5,000 members. It is dedicated to developing and maintaining the status of public-relations practice. Facilities include seminars, workshops, a journal and an extensive reference library. Student membership is open to those aged eighteen or over who are taking an IPR-recognized course of study leading to an examination in public relations. The IPR also provides an annual career seminar and careers counselling: if you send in your CV they will put you in touch with an experienced member to discuss Career prospects.

Institute of Sales Promotion
Arena House, 66–68 Pentonville Road, London N1 9HS
Telephone: 0171 837 5340

International Visual Communication Association
Bolsover House, 5–6 Clipstone Street, London W1P 8LD
Telephone: 0171 580 0962
Publishes a production handbook that lists film production and VNR companies.

Market Research Society
15 Northburgh Street, London
EC1V OAH
Telephone: 0171 490 4911
Can supply leaflets on market research industry qualifications and working as a market research interviewer.

The Outdoor Advertising Association
Fifth Floor, 77 Newman Street, London W1A 1DX
Telephone: 0171 637 7703
The trade association representing UK poster contractors. It publishes a brochure called *All You Ever Wanted to Know About Posters*.

Periodical Publishers Association
Imperial House, 15–19 Kingsway, London WC2B 6UN
Telephone: 0171 379 6268
Runs the Periodicals Training Council, which can provide a list of accredited colleges and information on careers within periodicals.

Public Relations Consultants Association (PRCA)
1st Floor, Willow House, Willow Place, Victoria, London SW1P 1JH
Telephone: 0171 233 6026
The PRCA represents PR consultancies, and has over 150 member companies, representing 80 per cent of the UK's public relations income.

Radio Advertising Bureau
74 Newman Street, London W1P 3LA
Telephone: 0171 636 5858

Register-MEAL
2 Fisher Street, London WC1R 4QA
Telephone: 0171 833 1212
Will provide data on advertising expenditure (broken down by brand, advertiser, sector, agency, etc.) to students free of charge. They normally ask for a copy of your student ID or a letter from your college as proof that you don't want the data for commercial purposes.

Skillset – The Industry Training Organization for Broadcast, Film & Video,
124 Horseferry Road, London SW1P 2TX
Telephone: 0171 306 8585
Can supply free information on training for film production.

Directories and Information Sources

BRAD
Short for *British Rate & Data*, published monthly by Emap Media. There are a couple of versions of this directory, one listing advertising information and contacts for British newspapers, another with data on consumer magazines, business titles, broadcast and outdoor media. It is prohibitively expensive for most individuals to subscribe to (over £500 a year) but copies can be found at many reference libraries. Subscriptions: 0181 242 3132/35.

Blue Book of British Broadcasting
Annual directory of all BBC, independent, cable and satellite media contacts, plus regional broadcasting maps, Subscriptions: 0171 490 1447.

Celebrity Service
A weekly digest that lists principal celebrities who are flying into Britain. Good for media 'celebrity bookers' and for PROs who want to publicize authors, actors and model clients. Subscriptions: 0171 439 9840.

Contact
Published by Haymarket, who also do *Campaign* and *PR Week*, *Contact* is an annual PR directory of services, in competition with the veteran directory *Hollis*. It is aimed primarily at senior in-house PR executives wishing to hire consultancy expertise. Cost £60. Subscriptions: 0171 413 4086.

Editors
A six-volume media directory covering national newspapers, radio and TV stations and news agencies, business and professional publications, provincial daily and weekly newspapers, consumer and leisure magazines, TV and radio programmes and writers' guilds, freelances and London correspondents of foreign press. Each volume is updated regularly. Subscriptions: 0171 251 9000.

Foresight
A crucial aspect of PR is ensuring that your event, launch or programme doesn't clash with anything else if possible and *Foresight* is the largest directory of events,

which highlights forthcoming dates and activities. Costs vary depending on types of service. Subscriptions: 0171 405 4455.

Guardian Media Guide

Annual, published in association with Fourth Estate. Lists all national and regional UK newspapers and newspapers groups, major broadcasters, media sources and outside contacts. Available in bookshops. Telephone: 0171 727 8993.

Hollis UK Press and Public Relations Annual

The industry bible for anyone in public relations or the media. It is a directory that lists press and PR contacts in key companies, organizations and industries, as well as listing every UK PR consultancy. *Hollis* also includes a section on sponsorship and event-management consultants. Discounts are available for IPR student members. Subscriptions: 01932 784781.

Hollis Europe

European edition of the *Hollis* directory. Subscriptions: 01923 784781.

London at Large

Similar to *Foresight* but only covers London. Costs vary for freelance and corporate users and types of service. Highly original and much recommended for any PR department Subscriptions: 0171 224 4464.

PIMS UK Media Directory

Publishes a variety of UK and European media directories, with updates on all contacts. Also available via an on-line service. Subscriptions: 0171 226 1000.

Programme News

Bi-monthly magazine, giving early information of planned and commissioned programmes in the broadcast media. Subscriptions: 0171 793 8220.

PR Newslink

A computerized media directory, updated daily, which lists every UK publication, station and programme prepared to accept and use a press release. Costs vary according to the systems you have. Subscriptions: 0171 251 9000.

PR Planner – UK and PR Planner – Europe

Directories of editorial contacts in the print and broadcast media, with regular updates. A familiar large orange binder in most PR departments and consultancies. Subscriptions: 0181 882 0155.

Targeter Gold

An on-line media database with contacts at over 18,000 different media outlets, including national and regional press, trade, technical and consumer magazines, plus radio and TV stations, specialist programmes and news and photo agencies. Available in an easy 'windows' format too. Mailing lists come out at the touch of a few buttons. Subscriptions: 0171 490 8111.

Writers' and Artists' Yearbook

Lists all publishers, agents and general media contacts. as well as useful reference for printing terms, etc. Subscriptions: 01480 212666.

Willings Press Guide

Vol. I: UK, Vol. II: Overseas. Reed Information services, East Grinstead, W. Sussex.

Trade Publications

Campaign (weekly)
Price £2.00. Subscriptions: 0181 845 8545.

International Public Relations Review
Published quarterly by the International Public Relations Association. PO Box 9588, Washington DC 20016, USA.

IPR Journal
Published by the Institute of Public Relations (IPR), ten issues per year. Subscriptions: 0171 253 5151.

Marketing (weekly)
Price: £1.90. Subscriptions: 0181 845 8545.

Marketing Week (weekly)
Price: £1.90. Subscriptions: 0171 292 3711.

Media Week (weekly)
Price: £1.85. Subscriptions: 0181 956 3016.

PR Week (weekly)
Price: £1.70. Subscriptions: 0181 845 8545.

UK Press Gazette (weekly)
Price: £1.50. Subscriptions: 01732 770823.

Chapter 13 / **Further Reading**

Advertising

Advertising, F. Jefkins (M+E Handbook)
Advertising: What it is and how to do it, R. White (McGraw-Hill)
The Complete Guide to Advertising, T. Douglas (Macmillan). Out of print but still available in many libraries.
Getting into Advertising, N. Staveley (The Advertising Association)
Marketing Communications, An Integrated Approach, P. Smith (Kogan Page)
Success in Advertising and Promotion, Don Milner (John Murray Publishers)

PR

The Essentials of Public Relations, Sam Black (Kogan Page, 1993)
Farewell to Hype: The Emergence of Real Public Relations, Francis Xavier Carty (Able Press, 1992)
The Marketer's Guide to Public Relations, Thomas L. Harris (John Wiley, 1993)
Public Relations Strategies and Tactics, Dennis L. Wilcox/Phillip H. Ault/Warren K. Agee (Harper Collins, US College Edition, 1995)
Public Relations, F. Jefkins (M+E Handbook 1992)
Public Relations Techniques, F. Jefkins (Butterworth Heinemann, 1994)
Making It In Public Relations, Leonard Mogel (Collier Books, 1993)
Successful Public Relations, Jim Dunn (Hawksmere, 1993)
Strategic Public Relations, ed. Norman A. Hart (Macmillan Business, 1995)
Winning PR Tactics, Peter Sheldon Green (Pitman, 1994)